Bear Market Baloney

Other books by Wade Cook:

<u>*Currently available in bookstores:*</u>
Wall Street Money Machine
Stock Market Miracles

Real Estate Money Machine
How To Pick Up Foreclosures
Real Estate For Real People
101 Ways To Buy Real Estate Without Cash

Wealth 101
Brilliant Deductions
Blueprints For Success
The Incorporation Handbook

<u>*Available from the publisher only:*</u>
Cook's Book On Creative Real Estate

<u>*Soon to be available at bookstores:*</u>
Business Buy The Bible
555 Clean Jokes

BEAR

MARKET

BALONEY

Wade B. Cook

Lighthouse Publishing Group, Inc.
Seattle, Washington

This publication is designed to provide accurate and authoritative information in regard to the subject matter covered. It is sold with the understanding that the publisher is not engaged in rendering legal, accounting, or other professional services. If legal or expert assistance is required, the service of a competent professional person should be sought. —*Adopted from a declaration of principles jointly adopted by a committee of the American Bar Association and committee of the Publishers' Association.*

Printed in the United States of America
10 9 8 7 6 5 4 3 2

Bear Market Baloney
ISBN: 0-910019-77-0
Library of Congress Cataloging-in-Publication Data in process

Book Design by Alison Curtis
Dust Jacket by Angela D. Wilson

Published by Lighthouse Publishing Group, Inc.

Wade Cook Financial, Inc.
ticker symbol WADE
14675 Interurban Avenue South
Seattle, Washington 98168
206-901-3000:phone
206-901-3100:fax

Distributed to the trade by Midpoint Trade Books, Inc.

No book is written or created in a vacuum. This book would not be what it is without the help of several people, Jerald Miller, Mark Engelbrecht, Alison Curtis, Angela Wilson, Connie Suehiro and, as always, Cheryle Hamilton. I appreciate the hard work each of these people put into this book.

Laura, my faithful wife, also deserves much recognition. Without her loving support and assistance, I would not be able to do what I do. Without her optimism and encouragement, I would not be the man that I am.

Contents

Preface

Baloney is such a strange word. It was listed twice in my dictionary. This first listing said it was a variation of bologna. I was expecting a rather large definition for the second listing, but it was not to be found. It said, simply, "nonsense." Not much else to say about that.

This book will not only explain my current feelings about the marketplace, but strategies and formulas to implement before, during, and after a small or large downturn in the market. I see so much bad news, listened to and watched by so many people, that I couldn't resist. With a passion I wrote, collected ideas, and put together this book. I have never acted so quickly. I wanted this information out to give hope, encouragement and actual "how to" advice on how to prosper.

One interesting side note was jockeying over the title. At first I wanted Bear Market Baloney. Then our publications department came up with Bear Market Bull-oney. This became the working title and I started showing the artwork around. I had to explain it every other time. Then a new title popped up: Bear Market: Bull Money, and while I think it is extremely clever, it too must be thought out, or explained.

Actually, I've had to explain the term "Bear Market" to quite a few people. I was dismayed at first but then enchanted later as I thought of this. There are countless people who do not know what a bull or bear market is. They have been through both, but didn't even know it.

All the variations on the word "baloney" were clever, and meaningful in a way. But alas, I had to get back to the word that meant what I wanted the title, indeed the book, to say.

One might get the impression I'm ignoring all the news, or pointing fingers. On the contrary, I want to use it to build cash flow. One might think I don't believe there will ever be another bear market. That is not what I think, nor what I've written in this book.

I will say it succinctly and without disclaimer: I think we are heading toward a bear market. There, are you happy? It seems everyone wants bad news.

Yes, there will be a bear market. There have always been dips, corrections, crashes, etc. BUT A BEAR MARKET IS NOT IMMINENT. There is plenty of time to make some real, "big time," money.

I'm projecting out one and a half to three years—basically the balance of this decade—this millennium, and I don't see a bear market. As baby boomers get older, trade barriers diminish, taxes come down a little (or are at least held in check), and the current good market could easily continue through 2005, and even to 2008, without a 1929 or 1987 crash.

Let's get to work. Let's keep things in perspective. Let's not give in to fear mongering by self-serving "money moguls." We don't need to put blinders on—we need to see all around us. Yes, let's get back to basics, and pick fundamentally great stocks to play. Yes, let's use aggressive strategies to build income, but use them sparingly. Yes, let's gamble on optimism. To all other negative emanations, let's just say, "Nonsense."

Common Abbreviations

Throughout this book, the author or others may refer to the names of other books or seminars. The following abbreviations may be used:

Brilliant Deductions	BD
Next STEP Seminar and/or Workshop	NS
Real Estate Money Machine	REMM
Stock Market Miracles	SMM
Wall Street Money Machine	WSMM
Wall Street Workshop	WSWS
Wealth Information Network (a BBS)	WIN

Other abbreviations that may be used:

Dow Jones Industrial Average	DJIA, DJ-30
General Agreement on Tariffs and Trades	GATT
National Association of Securities Dealers Automated Quotation System	NASDAQ
New York Stock Exchange	NYSE
Standard and Poors 500	S&P 500

Chapter 1

Not Now

Life is an illusion.
You are what you think you are.
—Yale Hirsch

I have, throughout this book, put together a collection of statements, transcriptions of public addresses, comments made in training sessions and on WIN (Wealth Information Network, our computer bulletin board service). My conclusions, made so often and based on different criteria at different times, have been relatively the same even as the current problem or question varied. However, the sum is a total of the parts and the parts say simply, "There will not be a bear market." Not now.

You, the reader, have a lot riding on how you perceive the market: where it's heading and how you're going to play it. To your stockbroker or financial planner (unless you find a rare one who really cares), the market going down probably will help the commission picture—there will be more people selling their positions to make commissions on, et cetera. But to you, it's the ham and egg example. The egg is a token donation for the chicken. The ham is "all there is" for the pig. You're in the pig's place. So, consider carefully all of the following comments and examples.

I don't think a bear market (one in the classical bear market sense) is about to happen. Might the market soften a little? Yes. Might there be temporary dips in the market and, more specifically, in a particular stock? Definitely yes.

My rationale for "not now" is not complicated and does not require a long thesis. Here it is:

1) There is no recession on the horizon.

2) Inflation is in check and the Federal Reserve is dedicated to keeping it there.

3) Corporate earnings are up everywhere. In some quarters, the only disappointing news is earnings coming in lower than what analysts expected. Ironic? Yes. Corporations are making millions, expanding sales, reducing debt, and growing, and then a $160 stock falls $8 in one hour because of 2¢ less reported earnings than expected.

> *People's spending habits depend more on how wealthy they feel than with the actual amount of their current income.*
> —A.S. Pigou

4) Taxes probably won't increase (at least directly) too much. There are too many conservatives hell-bent on lowering them to have much of a chance for increase. There might even be a capital gains tax reduction, which would be great—if only we can get some politicians to realize what a financial boon a reduction would create.

5) Interest rates will move up and down slightly in response to what the "Fed" perceives as inflationary.

6) Trade barriers are coming down worldwide. I don't care what your political persuasion is or how you view NAFTA and GATT (I personally don't agree with some of it, especially with some of the sovereignty

issues). These agreements, with more to follow, have stimulated trade.

a) The rest of the world needs so much of what we have. We are the world leader in:

Pharmaceuticals

Bio-technology

Hi-tech computers and all the peripherals: hardware, software, content and applications

Construction

And too many more to mention here.

Markets are currently in a state of uncertainty and flux and money is made by discounting the obvious and betting on the unexpected.
—*George Soros*

b) Way over half the world's population (some say 75% or more) are living in third world countries. Even the old Soviet Union and China qualify. There are countless "dollar-based" millionaires in these countries, and that, added to an exponentially growing middle class, bodes well for our products and services. (Note: India alone has a burgeoning middle class as large as the entire population of the United States.)

c) We can invest in these foreign companies or invest in American companies expanding into these new markets.

d) Expansion of existing products into new markets is a healthier prospect than developing new products for old markets. For example: McDonalds will do better opening up more stores in China than developing an octopus sandwich to sell in Kansas.

I'll deal with earnings more in several other places accompanied with strategies for making money, but in the theme of this section, "not now," I'd like to add a few thoughts:

There are definitely some companies' stocks with astronomical multiples—huge price/earnings ratios. These high prices usually won't be sustained unless the actual "drop-to-the-bottom-line" profits pick up—or raise to meet the high multiples. However, across the board of NYSE, NASDAQ, and S&P 500, multiples are not that high. Are they on the high side historically? Yes, a little. Have some retreated to more conservative levels? Yes, look at bank stocks, food stocks, et cetera.

Statements by high officials are practically always misleading when they are designed to bolster a falling market.
—Gerald Loeb

Many American companies are simply doing well. Management in most companies is in sync with customers and employees. Most are concerned with quality, which helps build a good expanding bottom line and great shareholder value.

When companies' multiples get really low, they become turnaround candidates and takeover/merger candidates. Many companies are on the prowl for new businesses which can add immediate earnings to their own bottom line.

Add all of this to the fact that so much of the world lies within reach and we have a triple whammy:

1) Low inflation.
2) No recession.
3) Good corporate earnings.

So, when will a bear market occur? I'm not a prognosticator. I don't know exactly when it will occur, but I do know two things:

1) It's not going to happen now or in the foreseeable future (say, one to four years). You should read *The Great Boom Ahead* by Harry S. Dent Jr. The author's research (consumer cycles, peaks) points to a current bull market ending around 2,007 or 2,008. His conclusions are based on baby boomers getting near retirement age. It's a convincing argument. I think if he errs, it is on the short end. Add to his calculations the "boomers" from Russia, China, and India growing older and adding to a worldwide expansion of commercialization, and you'll see why I say that.

> *It isn't as important to buy as cheap as possible as it is to buy at the right time.*
> —*Jesse Livermore*

2) You can tell the signs of a bear market before they happen. Think about it. If a bear market (however short and insignificant) is caused by certain factors: high interest rates (which could have occurred by a Fed worrying about inflation and which could end with lower corporate earnings occurring simultaneously or close to each other) high taxes, high inflation, and low corporate earnings; and if a bull market is caused by the opposite (low interest rates, relatively low taxes, lower inflation, and good earnings) then the answer is simple: watch for real moves—up or down—in these areas. I say real because the Fed might tinker with rates in response to fears (not actual occurrences) of things they think are important.

The horizon would need to have all three clouds (a storm if you will) coming together. My solution: keep an eye on the horizon but get busy making money. Make hay while the bull climbs.

How? Read on.

Chapter 2

Bear-ly Noticeable

*Average earnings of an English worker in 1900
came to half an ounce of gold a week and,
in 1979, after world wars, a world slump,
and a world inflation, the British worker has
an average earnings of half an ounce of gold a week.*
—William Rees Mogg

It is difficult to keep things in perspective. At the time of the crash of 1987, there were too many comparisons to 1929 to even count. Charts pointed out the likeliness and the likelihood of the two events. Cyclists developed 50-year cycles, 12-year cycles, 4-year cycles, and so on. There were political observers and economists everywhere, each with his or her own theory.

Yes, it is true, there are several similarities between the two events. And yes, there are numerous attempts to make sense or figure out what happened—maybe an attempt to pigeonhole the phenomena made it understandable and hence, palatable. I reject most of these attempts.

The only thing I agree with is this: a set of circumstances occur in no particular order. A cause (however minor) starts and a chain reaction commences. The situation, usually totally irrationally, takes on a life of its own. The crash (or whatever you want to call it) ends for different reasons, and the recovery time period and strengths are totally unrelated.

*The worst
bankrupt in the
world is
the person who
has lost his
enthusiasm.*
—H.W. Arnold

A strange, but hopefully useful, comparison would be Woodstock. I was not there. I was too busy with my own rock-and-roll band. The place, the timing, the participants, the attendees, what preceded the event, the feelings at the event and afterward created "Woodstock." Many attempts have been made to recreate the main event. Thirty years later, one was pulled off that would, in a few ways, parallel the original event. The point being, it is a phenomenon that can't be recreated. It just happens. I'm sure everyone reading this has had such an event. Maybe a honeymoon, a vacation, a special meeting, whatever. Attempts to duplicate it are futile.

So that's what I'd like to accomplish here: give a comparison of the 1929 and 1987 crash, not to prove that they were the same, but to prove that they were not the same. I won't purposefully try to discount any comparisons which match up. I won't have to. You'll see that any likeness usually had different timing and effects.

Why do I make this attempt? Only to educate others so that readers, my seminar attendees, and even my staff will not make decisions based on incomplete or erroneous information. This comparison will be relatively short. It would serve you well to study greater and more comprehensive studies of this matter. History may not recreate itself, but if we don't study history, we are destined to repeat ourselves.

The 1929 Crash:
The roaring twenties were hardly a crash to Main Street. People were working, factories were humming,

and a new religious revival was happening. Speakeasies were around, but were not the norm.

The buildup to 1929, and even the first half of that year, had progressed at a fairly rapid pace. Many average Americans were buying stocks. Mutual funds were many years in the future, as were derivatives of stocks, like options and other interest rate, index-related securities. But margin investing did exist and was used extensively. The Dow Jones Industrial Average peaked on September 3rd. It turned around, however, and in the first two weeks of October, it rallied to 353.

> *The worse a situation becomes, the less it takes to turn it around, the bigger the upside.*
> —*George Soros*

News happens. On October 15th, the Weekly Production figures came in and US Steel was down 17%. Heavy selling commenced. Back then, the market had a Saturday trading session. US Steel fell $27.75 that week. General Electric and other stocks were down. Obviously, everyone was concerned. A group of big banks got together immediately and committed one billion dollars to bolster the market. This worked, as the market temporarily stopped skidding.

On October 24th, one million shares traded in just 30 minutes. Buyers couldn't be found and major companies' stock (even the most previously liquid stock) plunged— sometimes dipping $5 to $10 between trades. That day 12.9 million shares traded. The old one-day record was 8.2 million.

The *Wall Street Journal* added fuel to the fire. On Monday, October 28th, its headline read, "Stock Market

Crisis," and sales orders poured in even before the market opened.

Tuesday, the market fell another 30 points. It closed at 261. It was at 381 on September 3rd, and had fallen 31%. General Motors was at $40 from its high that year of $91.75. General Electric had been $422, now it bottomed at $222.

How could the bad news from US Steel cause a crash? It didn't, but was one log on the fire. No one factor caused the crash. A culmination of events, news, and statements, created a selling atmosphere which eventually created a crash.

Consider:

Earnings were okay. They surely didn't seem to be heading lower. Many companies and many experts were looking to a good solid growth pattern extending through 1930. Chrysler shipped 17,000 more cars in 1929 than 1928. Household furnishing orders were up. Typewriter sales were up. Many other companies showed increased earnings on the horizon.

No matter how little you've done in life, how much you've abused yourself, whatever your lifestyle or your occupation, you can improve.
—Nolan Ryan

Were stocks expensive? Not in general. Some were, and their high multiples were based on projected future earnings. This is not uncommon. All in all, stocks just didn't seem high priced based on the future. But, on current earnings per share, they were high. For example, General Electric's high of $403 was at price to earnings ratio of 56, or 56 times earnings. See **Stock Market Miracles** and **Wall Street**

Money Machine for more on the importance of price to earnings ratios.

When excitement builds and people don't want to get left out, they'll do anything to get in. They'll borrow heavily—home mortgages, personal loans, etc. Margin accounts, at brokerage firms were at an all time high. Some allowed investors to put up as little as 10%. Obviously, a downturn would hurt, and they assured extra selling.

Think of it. As stock slides a little, the investor has to cover the collateral by bringing in more stocks or cash. In a full fall, they could not cover, and mass selling occurred to stop further erosions. Another log on the fire.

If you destroy a free market you create a black market. If you have ten thousand regulations you destroy all respect for the law.
—Winston Churchill

Interest rates were high. Just before September, the Federal Government raised its discount rates from 5% to 6%. This was the fourth rise in rates from 1927. They were raised to stem the flow of gold out of the country. With this negative economic news, foreign investors sold US stocks and bonds before they continued to erode.

Now to another bugaboo, another large log. Congress seemed likely to pass a very restrictive tariff bill, virtually isolating American industries, restricting their ability to trade freely (or at least less restrictively). Like now, it seems out-bungling politicians can't seem to get government out of our pockets, causing more harm than good. The *Wall Street Journal* reported this story on October 28th. It was the Smoot-Hawly Tariff Bill, a bill so damaging in the cause and length of the Great Depression.

All of these factors together added up to the crash of 1929. No one thing caused it.

The Biggest Crash In History, 1987:

The 1987 stock market crash was incredible. The recovery took nowhere near as long as the 1929 crash, but in terms of dollars, its loss was more severe. The market once again turned expensive. Just like 1929, certain specific events led up to the crash. You'll see, except for stock prices being high, no event listed here is the same as 1929.

On October 14th, the Dow Jones Industrial average went down 95 points. This set a new record. Why? News came out that the trade deficit for August was $10 billion. This caught people by surprise.

Then the House Ways and Means Committee set about to change the tax filing requirements for mergers between big companies. Such mergers or acquisitions had failed to produce some of the expected price/value increases, and this tax change was seen to have damaging consequences. That Thursday, the Dow Jones Industrial average fell 58 points. The next day, it fell another 108 points. It stood at 2,247: 17% less. A decline from its high on August 25th. Too many logs too fast.

The mass of men lead lives of quiet desperation.
—Henry David Thoreau

Monday saw a panic. The Dow dropped 508 by the close, going down in major chunks all day long. An astounding number of shares traded that day. I owned stocks at that time, but was so busy running my business, I hardly noticed. When I did, I bought more shares.

Was the 1987 crash like 1929 in its severity? Yes. But in its causes, not hardly, except for a few things. Stocks were priced high. In August, for example, the S&P 500 traded at 25 times earnings.

Investors and analysts (brokers) were finding innovative justifications for purchasing stocks at these high prices. One such valuation was modern in nature. It's called "break-up value." Buy a company, even with expensive debt, then sell off divisions, or assets, pay off the debt and pocket the excess. Mergers and acquisitions abounded. Anyone who held onto stocks through the '80s was much better off even after the 30% decline because shareholder value had increased so much.

In 1929, margin usage had been overused. New margin requirements were 50%. However, new forms of "margin" popped up. One was index futures, and options. This allowed investors with small amounts of money to tie up larger positions. The "magnified" movement on these derivatives can make overnight millionaires or overnight paupers.

The test of success is not what you do when you are on top. Success is how high you bounce when you hit bottom.
—General George S. Patton

Another thing occurred in 1985 and 1986. The Federal Reserve (under Paul Volcker) expanded the money supply, up 12% in 1985 and 16% in 1986. This easy money found its way to the stock market. Inflation seemed guaranteed and interest rates were just starting to increase. Stocks seemed like the place to be. Many investors bought in.

Mutual fund investing saw billions of dollars pour in from individual investors

In the realm of ideas, everything depends on enthusiasm, in the real world, all rests on perseverance.
—Goethe

who "trusted" these big fund managers more than their own instincts. This money had to be invested.

Just like in 1929, the Federal Government's monetary policy shifted two months before the crash. This time it was Alan Greenspan. He replaced Paul Volcker and, on September 3rd, raised the discount rate from 5.5% to 6%.

The dollar started falling and it now required foreign investors to finance our debt. The amount of foreign involvement dropped in half. Now, this increase in the interest rates would draw foreign investors back into the game.

After the crash, the Federal Government announced it would provide whatever liquidity the market needed to stem the tide. The market rebounded 150 points by December 31st.

The only really significant comparison is that stocks seemed overpriced. So, this should also be our concern. No single event caused it. Neither wars, impeachments, corporate bankruptcies, nor tragedies of any sort have sent the markets into decline. Crashes are not random events. They occur when a series of negative things happen which affect or infect investor attitudes.

No one knows when, but you will read elsewhere in this book how you can watch the horizon, diversify, stay with some cash and learn how to play any type of market.

Chapter 3

Bear-ly Believable

I'm a great believer in luck,
and I find the harder I work the more I have of it.
—Thomas Jefferson

I teach a simple concept in my real estate seminars: the road to wealth is not a freeway. It has many ups and downs, many detours, and many pot holes along the way. The stock market in general, and any single stock in particular, is the same way. You can get a historical chart of any company and you will see a line that looks like the outline of a jagged mountain range, sometimes going up to new highs—the peaks getting higher and the lows become higher as well. Or the complete opposite is true. A stock has three choices: it is either going up, down, or sideways.

As I teach in my live Wall Street Workshops and Next Step seminars, we need to take advantage of the volatility of stocks. I know this is the key to so much of what goes on in the "generating cash flow" aspect of the stock market. Volatility is important, especially on a quick-turn basis. Whether we're playing the stock or an option on the stock (either a call option which gives us the right to buy or a put option which gives us the right to sell) we are going to take advantage of the turning point of the stock when it reaches a peak or a valley. I've covered this extensively in a chapter called Quick Turn Profits in *Stock Market Miracles*. I will not belabor the point here except to say that this is where a lot of money can be made. We should look at volatility as our friend, not as our enemy.

Many factors enter into the picture and determine when a stock is going to bottom out or when it's going to hit its top. There have been so many companies hitting new highs lately and then, within a month or two, hitting new highs again. There are many plays along the way, many chances to make money. You can almost bet when a company hits a new high—especially if it "gaps up" (meaning that it opens up substantially higher than it closed the day before)—there is a chance to make money on the way back down. Then when a stock goes down and hits its support level, there is still another chance to make money on the way back up. A stock may test its support several times and when it does so—and as the news starts to change and the stock starts to move back up—there is another opportunity to make money.

Money makes money.
And the money that money makes makes more money.
—*Benjamin Franklin*

One of my favorite ways of making money on these dips is to sell puts on the stock, agreeing to buy the stock at a certain price. I do this when I want to take the stock. I also do this when I don't want to take the stock but I just want to pick up the Put premium. I agree to take the stock, but with the hope that the stock is going to rise and the premium will go down and I can either buy the Put option back at a lower price or just go ahead and let it expire and keep all the money. I also buy Call options when the stocks are low. I can then sell Call options when the stock is high. So, there are many strategies to utilize the volatility of these stocks.

Now let's move on and talk about the market in general. How do we make ourselves aware of different major dips in the market place and how do we protect ourselves against them? Here are some thoughts:

1) As I've said in other places in this book, there are tell-tale signs of when a recession is going to occur. There are also signs of when there's going to be a major market dip. However, most of us will never see those because, as small investors, we do not have access to some of the things that the big-time traders have. For example, program traders have a sell order written into the computer for when funds hit a certain level, or for a stock within a fund which hits a certain level (this is true for several funds, including retirement funds and mutual funds) . They also have a sell order written that activates when a certain percentage of profits are made. Likewise, when a stock hits a certain price, they place purchase orders for when it goes down.

Luck is the preparation for, recognition of, and proper seizure of opportunity.

—Walter Heiby

This type of trading, especially rapid program trading on the sell side, can cause a major dip in the marketplace. After much research on the 1987 crash, I think this was probably the major cause for the crash. Yes, the stocks were running up right before that and there was a nice rapid bull market in the summer and fall of 1987. All this led to a lot of profit taking. Once the selling started, it was almost a panic. Within a day there were millions upon millions of shares being sold by people who wanted to take their profits or who were caught up in the herd mentality. A huge momentum downward in the stock market resulted.

And within a day or two the stock market crashed almost 30%. If you think about it, 30% of the value of companies is like letting air out of a tire, it has to hit a support level eventually. It did within a couple of days. And the climb back up started almost immediately. It was a major opportunity for a lot of people to take advantage of that serious correction.

2) I believe that corrections, whether they're mini or maxi, are necessary. They shake out a lot of the people who are just in it for the ride and are not serious investors in any particular company. The negativism caused by that stops companies from having hyper-inflated prices. As I mentioned elsewhere, the bears will always be with us and they are necessary to keep everything in check. So, we observe the bear market mentality and play it from the opposite side.

Buy a stock the way you would buy a house. Understand and like it such that you'd be content to own it in the absence of any market.
—Warren Buffett

3) Diversification is also important. Not only should we have a lot of our money tied up in really good solid investments like blue chip stocks and good mutual funds, we should also be looking to buy stocks which perform well in recessions and perform well when the stock market is going down. Brokers call these stocks "negative beta down" stocks.

There are other measuring sticks which point the way to stocks that perform well in these kind of market places, too. If you do have a high need for safety and security in your stock market investments, you should consider buying these types of stock. If you fear the rapid volatility of a crash, you may want to avoid options. Or, when the stock does start to fall, you may want to buy Put options, ride a stock price down, and gain value in your Put option as the stock falls.

4) If you do invest in options in a particular stock you could do short term plays and long term plays. I have outlined these in numerous courses and numerous books. You should buy a short term option at or near the strike price or "slightly in the money" Call options. Buy further out options, say 4, 5, or 6 months out, and go one or two strike prices above just to give yourself some safety (to have backup hedge on your option plays). However, I do not want to make it sound like that is going to be a panacea remedial action for everything that's going to happen. If there is a huge 10%, 20%, or 30% crash in the market-place, virtually all of your options would be worthless and probably not recover in time. That's why you go back to point number three: you should diversify and not have a lot of your money tied up in riskier option plays.

The word "crises" in Chinese is composed of two characters: the first, the symbol of danger; the second, opportunity.
—Anonymous

Here's an example. Look at July of 1996. I had a small percentage of my portfolio, around $40,000, tied up in options. Now, I had made several hundred thousand dollars, but I lost around $30,000 on July 16th of 1996, when the stock market took a crash. Look at the timing of this crash. This was not that serious of a crash. If you look at the chart for the balance of the year, you can see that the stock market recovered and went way above where it was before the correction in the marketplace. However, on a short term basis, there was not any way our options could recover—especially the July options—before the expiration date.

That serious dip occurred just a few days before the July expiration date. We were sitting pretty on some of those options on Monday. On Tuesday—the day of the dip—they went down and almost became worthless. They did not recover by that Friday. So all the options we could have sold on Monday (either breaking even or making a profit) we lost money on, and in just a few days. Nobody knew this was coming. It just happened one day, due to lot of program trading going on, and a lot of sentiment built into the marketplace.

5) I've repeatedly said this, but these types of corrections are not only necessary but good. When the "sky is falling" (i.e. people start saying the stock market is too high), they do have their day. Once in awhile the market can take a serious dip in a day, but usually the information that causes these corrections is discounted almost before it ever happens. This is especially true when a major firm is downgrading certain stocks or making comments about the market place in general, or we have a comment by Allen Greenspan or another influential person. Wise people and people who've been around for a long time know that ebbs and flows can turn into ebbs and cash flows. That's what I've tried to teach at all my seminars and in my books.

Good judgement is usually the result of experience and experience frequently is the result of bad judgement.
—Robert Lovell

6) Don't panic. If there is a major correction in the market place you will be well served to be very, very patient. Especially

with modern day trading as compared to the 1929 crash, which did not cause the recession but preceded the recession of 1932. In today's economy, stock market setups have huge mutual funds, program trading, and all the technical analysis that has become much more sophisticated than before. They are set to defend against sudden, serious dips. Yes, history might repeat itself. Yes, there are certain cycles that may be valid. However, there's nothing that will substitute for good solid homework: checking the fundamentals of a company, investing our money in good solid companies having the highest likelihood for improved earnings, making a good return, earning a lot of money, and increasing the earnings. This is where we should be putting most of our money. If our money is there, a slight correction in the marketplace, or even a serious correction, should not shake us from our underlying premise.

Chance favors the informed mind.
—Louis Pasteur

Now, don't get me wrong. We need to check the storyline of each company and if the storyline has changed—if the company is not profitable anymore—we may want to unload and get our money into investments having the highest likelihood of making money. I have tried to make sure that I am not emotionally involved in any particular company. Yes, I have the companies I like—Nordstroms, Disney and several other huge companies. Nevertheless, even though I like owning those stocks, I would sell them in a minute. I learned this training in my real estate days. Don't get too involved in a particular property because, when you do, you start making stupid decisions. You should not base your decisions for buying a stock, holding a stock, or selling a stock on any emotional factors at all. It should be done on pure simple mathematics and the best calculation as to how you can make the greatest return possible.

*All you need is to look over the earnings
forecasts publicly made a year ago to see
how much care you need to give those
being made now for the next year.*
—Gerald Loeb

In conclusion: The stock market seems to do whatever it takes to make fools out of most people most of the time. In many ways, there's no way to figure out the exact timing of any move in the market place. What we can do to protect ourselves is to stay diversified, have our money in good investments, and treat aggressive plays for exactly what they are—using only our extra money or money that can be invested and put at risk. Only use money we could lose and not feel too badly about.

We need to become not only generalized observers of the marketplace but also specific observers of the stocks we're following. On the road to wealth, we just got to take advantage of the bumps and dips. And, hopefully, enjoy the beautiful scenery along the way.

Chapter 4

Bad News Bears

The greatest trouble with most of us is that our demands upon ourselves are so feeble, the call upon the great within us so weak and intermittent that it makes no impression upon the creative energies.
—Orlson Swett Marden

There is a fundamental flaw in the way most people think about success in business or success in their career. People think there's a major difference between a great company and a not-so-great company or even a bad company. Those of us who have been in business for a long time realize this is just not the case. The major difference between a great company and the next to great or barely great, is often just one or two extra sales.

Again, if you've had your own business, one or two extra sales a week could make the difference of whether your business makes it or not. If you have large items for sale, one or two extra sales a month could literally determine whether you have the money to make payroll or not. It's that extra little effort, that extra 110% or 200% that some people put out. Having a couple of really great salespeople among all the mediocre people who are out there can make the difference. Having people who believe success can be had and strive for it makes all of the difference. It is tough enough to make it in business without negativism entering the picture.

Let's relate this to stock market investing. You've got to realize there's going to be negativism.

- A lot of people make their living from being negative. There is a whole cottage industry built up of newsletters and seminars that dwell on people's fears. They try to get people overly concerned with bad things in life. I'm reminded of a story of a lady who was sitting in a seminar about environmental concerns in California. She got really excited and started saying to the speaker, "What, what, what did you say? What did you just say there about the San Andrea's Fault? What did you say about earthquakes?" And the speaker said, "Well I said that there is probably going to be a major earthquake in the next billion years." And she says, "Oh, oh, billion years. Shhhheeeewww. I'm really glad you said that because I thought I heard you say a million years." I hope you get the point. A lot of people are worrying about things they should not be worrying about.

The facts are unimportant! It's what they are perceived to be that determines the course of events.
—R. Earl Haday

- There are so many people who get petty: tripping over pennies on their way to dollars, thinking negative and small thoughts when none are warranted or justified.

- It seems that the daily barrage of media attacks on anything positive has had a major impact on a lot of people's lives. It seems like you can't open up a newspaper anywhere where there are two columns of good information side by side. I know we have become a nation of ambulance chasers. You see these violent news reports and movies and, as long as there are a lot of bad things going on, people will watch. I guess it is true that a news report about good information would not be well watched or popular. As long as there is negative news about inflation and interest rates, people will watch. But can you imagine a news report saying something like this: "Well, while all of you were at work today your house went up in value. Yes, the good news is the econ-omy is doing well and your stock portfolio has now increased. You're one step closer to being able to put your child through college."

A statistician is someone who can draw a straight line from an unwar-ranted assump-tion to a foregone conclusion.
—Anonymous

But we don't hear anything like this. It is always the negative. And the more we hang around the negative and the more we are barraged by it, the more of an impact it has on our lives and the more we have to fight to counter it. So what do we do?

Let me give you several things that I think will help you make money in this kind of negative atmosphere.

1) Consider the source. What is the person dissemi-nating the negative information trying to accom-plish? What are they trying to get out of this? More specifically, what are they trying to sell? If it's a newsletter, if it's a negative position in the stock mar-ket like a short sell or buying puts, then fine—just know what they're trying to get out of it. I'm not say-ing that it's right or wrong, just what is everybody going to get out of this deal? Now you'll understand this!

2) Why not use this negativism as a barometer to help you decide when to sell different stocks and options? Let me give you a scenario. The stock market does not climb on an even basis. You would not look at it and say it is an even set of steps going up. Not only are the height and the width of the steps unequal, but the length of them (the timing of them) is not equal.

As the stock market moves up there are always going to be dips. In *Wall Street Money Machine* I call these "Range Riders." A stock will start at $20 and go up to $24, but then back off to $22, and then go up to $26, and then back off to $23. Then it will go up to $26 1/2 and back off to $24. It may be two or three weeks or even two or three months between these dips, but as a stock rises, as a company is expanding, as its earnings are growing, a lot of market sentiment enters the picture. It is to this point that I'm trying to address these remarks.

The market is a voting machine, whereon countless individuals register choices which are the product partly of reason and partly of emotion.
—Graham & Dodd

Why not use this market sentiment? The market is not only not always right, but it is usually wrong. People cause changes. We are all participants in the marketplace whether we are actually buying stocks or mutual funds or just shopping at K-Mart or Sears. We are participants in the marketplace and, being participants. It is hard to sit back and watch it because everything we do, whether we're buying a stock or selling a stock or any other activity related to this, affects the pricing of the stock. Yes, its effects may be small, but there is a significance to all of our moves. Now, taken together, we are considered the market. There is a lot of market mentality or market sentiment that enters the picture.

When the stock market rises on good economic news or the fact that the Chairman of the Federal Reserve is not going to raise interest rates and the stock market rallies 80 or 90 points, you most assuredly know that in the next few days that 80 or 90 points are going to be given back. Maybe not all of it, but quite a bit, say 70 points.

Likewise, when there is either a rumor of bad economic news or actual bad economic news and the stock market takes a dip, it's probably going to get back most of what it lost within the next few days. It's almost as if what Monday giveth, Tuesday taketh away. And what Tuesday taketh away, Friday giveth back.

> *In a bull market, an "overbought" condition lasts longer while an "oversold" condition ends very quickly. The reverse is true in bear markets.*
> *—Alan R. Shaw*

I know it's not exactly that simplistic, but it almost looks that simplistic when you look at historical charts. It may not be on a day-to-day basis where it goes up 80 points one day and down 80 points the next day. However, when you see a dip in the market place, why not play it as it goes back up?

If you're using the Dow Jones Industrial Average, that's 30 stocks with a lot of trading going on. These stocks are on a weighted average. It's hard to tell how much impact any one particular stock has on the whole, but if IBM has a serious dip for one day, it is definitely going to take the Dow Jones Industrial Averages down. If the Dow Jones Industrial Average goes down 80 or 90 points in one day, why not look into it? Find the two, three, or four stocks that have gone down and buy the stocks or options on the stocks and ride them back up. See, sometimes you can make intra-day trades and catch a dip either in a particular stock or in the market as a whole. Sometimes it takes a little longer. Either way, you can make money.

I'm reminded continually of this when I have people coming through our live Wall Street Workshops. It's almost like a direct challenge is given to me or to our instructors: "Well, the stock market is down 90 points today." They want to see what we'll do. Sometimes, this happens as we get there in the morning at 6:30. The stock market takes a big dip or opens up down 40 or 50 points. They're thinking that all hell is going to break loose and the sky is falling once again. Then, we turn around and the stock market is down another 40 points, we jump in on a few stocks, and the Dow Jones, within an hour and a half, is up 30 points. Then two hours later, it's down 60 points, and later, it's up 29 points again. So there's a lot of intra-day trades which can be made. And these can be especially profitable if you're playing options.

> *Without development there is no profit, without profit, no development.*
> —Joseph A. Schumpeter

3) If you are going to play options, there are special concerns. Options are very risky, in that they are fixed time investments. When you look at the charts and diagrams of these different plays and strategies you need to make sure that you buy an option out far enough. You do the best guess timing you possibly can. For example, if a particular stock goes down from $93 to say $85 in one day, then you have to look and say, "Well, why is this stock

down? Is the whole market down or is this stock down because of news about the particular stock?"

And, if the stock is down but the whole market is up, that tells you there may be a negative trend and you ought to be calling your stockbroker and asking about the news of the stock. Conversely, if the stock is up and the whole market is down, that could signify very good strength in the company. However, the point is that you're trying to catch the stock at either at a new high, or a bottom (support level).

> *Quality is never an accident; it is always the result of high intention, genuine effort, intelligent direction, and skillful execution.*
> —*Willa A. Foster*

Very seldom does a stock hit a high and then hit a high the next day and the next day and then continue. At some point, usually within a week after its new high, it's going to back off. It may not be down to the point where it was before it ran up to the high, but it's definitely going to back off a little. Now, whether you're going to buy Puts on a "peaked out" stock, or buy Call options on a dip in the stock, you still need to do them out far enough, at least a full month, but usually two to four months, so that you can weather any vicissitudes in the stock.

4) Don't bet your money on one particular option. Not only should you be diversified in investing smaller amounts of money in many different options on many different stocks, but also within the same stock you should be looking at different strike prices, different expiration months and most importantly different purchase points. For example, let's say a stock has gone from $93 down to $85 and you go

ahead and buy the option. Let's assume that it's June and you buy the August $85 call option for $4 and the stock goes down to $83. Now the $80 call option for August is $4. I hate to use the words "averaging down," but you can get involved at many different price points. When it takes another dip, you could buy more options at a lower price, or later options, giving you more time for the same price, and then wait for it to come back up from $80 to $85. You may want to buy the October or November options at a higher strike price so that it won't take so much money. Then, as they increase in value, sell and take your profits.

Unless you've interpreted changes before they've occurred you'll be decimated trying to follow them.
—Robert J. Nurock

The point is that there are many different plays and many times to get involved. At no point in time should you be investing all of your money into one option, one strike price and one month on one particular company. Diversification is the key in this case.

Let's use negative, even intra-day, comments as a way to watch trends. I'm saying we should not be too involved in the particular movements of the stock unless we are really trying to play quick turn options. I have a whole section on that type of transaction in *Stock Market Miracles*. For now, we should be looking at the market as a whole—catching the trend of the market place.

If you look at the market as a whole over the past _____ (you fill in the blank, it won't matter how many you choose) years, you'll notice there's been an upward trend. The average compounded returns over the years has been about 16%. I know my students who have attended the Wall Street Workshop are doing far superior to that. Sometimes getting 16% in a week or two (not annual returns). You can definitely look at the trends by looking at the comments every day.

Let's go back to the intra-day trades and see if we can look at the comments that happen either on a weekly or monthly basis, comments from newspapers and newsletters. If you hear many people saying that the market is either going to crash or the stock prices are too high, then look at the particular stocks you are following and see if what they're saying is relevant.

Buy on the rumor, sell on the news.
-*Market Maxim*

For example, imagine you have a stock that you bought around $70 and it has slowly climbed up to $77. Now, on merger information or good news coming out about its earnings, the stock pops up to $92. At $92 everybody is saying that not only is the market going to crash but this stock is way overpriced. Just the fact that a lot of people are talking negative about this company will have a very dramatic and negative impact, and usually a very quick impact, on the company's stock. This could get even more pronounced if several of the major brokerage houses are recommending this stock as a strong buy, and all of a sudden change their recommendation.

Rationalize this one through with me: brokers still like the stock but they liked it better when it was at $70. Now that it's at $92 they need to look at it once again. The stock has gone from a <u>strong</u> buy to a buy or to a hold. The stock has risen to a point where they will not recommend to their clients that they should buy the stock at $92. If that is the case, a lot of people will perceive (and that's all it is, a perception, usually by naive people), that this company's stock may not be good anymore. You'll have a whole lot of selling going on. At least it will stop the run-up.

You may be better to go ahead and sell your stock at $92 and pick it up again at $82 or $85 after the shakeout occurs. This is basically trying to stay ahead of the herd, but if you can't get ahead of the herd, follow the herd only to a certain extent. Yes, yes, yes, yes. There may be many momentum investors. When the stock hits $92 they start jumping in because they see all the activity. So you may want to look again at the balance of power in the stock, the difference between the volume of buying and selling.

Many charting services give this information. Try to find out about the cash going into the stock as compared to the cash going out of the stock. Basically, it's the number of buyers and the numbers of shares being sold as compared to the number of shares being purchased and at what prices. So the balance of power (how much buying and selling is going on) can be a good indication whether $92 is a top. You may want to hang around just a little bit more and ride it from $92 to $94, but at some point in time, all the negative information is going to pan out and become real. Instead of just a report about the stock, it will become actual selling.

Successful investing is anticipating the anticipations of others.
—John Maynard Keynes

I think at this point in time you would have rather sold the stock at $92 than to have had it run up, even within an hour or the next day, to $94, then backed off to $88 before the day is over. So again, don't get greedy. Realize that on any particular run up in the stock there will be many people who will come out of the woodwork and start bad mouthing the company. More particularly, they will start bad mouthing the price range that the stock is currently in. Even though the company may be really well run and solid fundamentally, the negative talk may drive down the price of the stock.

To wrap this section up, we want to take any of the bad market sentiments and use them to our advantage. We don't want to be an ostrich with our head in the sand, but we also don't want to overreact to negative and pull ourselves out of the marketplace.

Don't compete. Create. Find out what everyone else is doing and then don't do it.
—Joel Weldon

We should use negative talk to time our entry into the market place on any particular stock: to choose a very, very wise and good time to get involved. My feeling is that, while the true bears are not always going to be with us in the same numbers as of late, there will always be negative people who are always there and are overly vocal—no matter what happens. Also, there are always people who look at the same market statistics and numbers, and the same economic factors but interpret them a different way.

From my experience, there are just negative people and they do have a negative impact. Because they are always there does not mean that what they say is always true. As a matter of fact, it's almost impossible to find a "bear-sayer" who has been right two quarters in a row. In the last five to eight years, they have been so badly off target that they hardly have any credibility. It is at this point in time that we want to be careful. With the market rising, the bears may have a tendency to shut up, but we want them there. They cause movement and volatility and keep us from complacency.

Do your work with your whole heart and you will succeed— there is so little competition.
—Elbert Hubbard

We want them saying their negative things. If you follow the Wade Cook stock market strategies, we thrive on volatility, we profit from quick turns, bottoms, peaks, and other "newsy" moves. Whether the strategy is Range Riders, Rolling Stocks, or Reverse Range Riders for our stock plays and our mutual fund plays, or stock splits, etc., for our quick turn option plays, we need a lot of buying enthusiasm going on when stocks take a dip; we also need a lot of selling enthusiasm going on when stocks rise to unprecedented heights. I'm into "irrational exuberance."

What you're going to do with this depends on where you are personally. Are you positive or are you negative? Do you play the positive side of the market or do you play the negative side of the market? I contend that you should not gamble on pessimism. You should definitely not throw all your eggs in the basket of optimism, but if you're going to err, err on the side of the stock market going up, of companies continuing to thrive, of companies continuing to expand overseas, and of companies trying to bring more value to their shareholders. Err on the positive side, and you'll err less often.

Chapter 5

Load Bear-ing

*Knowledge born from actual experience is
the answer to why one profits;
lack of it is the reason one loses.*
—Gerald Loeb

Buying and selling options to purchase stock are simple strategies loaded with opportunities regardless of the direction of the market. The only inherent risk of options is that they expire. However, they can generate fantastic returns in a relatively short amount of time. This is because option prices move up and down with the price of the stock, but on an exaggerated level. If you haven't already read my books on stock market strategies, I suggest you do so soon. *Wall Street Money Machine* and *Stock Market Miracles* are loaded with detailed, step-by-step outlines of each strategy that I have tried and tested myself to ensure maximum returns with minimum risk. Following is a very brief synopsis of some of those strategies. Remember, when you buy or sell an option, you buy or sell the right, not necessarily the obligation, to buy the underlying stock.

My favorite ways of making money have several things in common.

1) They are definitely about cash flow—actual money hitting the account.

2) They generate cash quickly—usually every two to six weeks.

3) They lend themselves to duplication. My motto is: "Don't do anything which can't be duplicated," sung to the tune of "I'd rather lose money and know how I lost it, than make money and not know how I made it." But I'll never lose money for long.

4) They are easy to understand—I love teaching strategies and plays that I, a former cab driver, and most of my students can do.

5) The downside risk is mitigated: the risk is lessened either by the inherent nature of the strategy, or by all the cautions I've built into the particular way I use the formulas.

6) Most can be done in a "tax free environment." This is difficult for many people to understand. Some people have heard of tax free investments, like a municipal bond, but most have not heard of a tax free entity which makes all forms of investing tax free (Keogh Plans, IRA's, SEP IRA's, 401K's and the best, a Corporate Pension Plan).

7) The strategies and formulas almost become self perpetuating.

My staff and I teach eleven different cash flow strategies at the Wall Street Workshop. Most of these are covered in my books—not with the same vivacity of actually doing deals, but at least covered. A very brief glance at a few of the 11 strategies are listed here. Variations of these plays will help build cash flow, help you purchase additional growth or cash flow assets, and will help you mitigate any damage done by a bear market.

Wade's Strategies:

Bottom Fishing:

This is a simple way of finding stocks which are severely underpriced, or at least ones which you think have a high likelihood for going much higher.

Stocks in this category could come from:

- Really bad news.
- Bankrupt (Chapter 11) companies on their way out of bankruptcy.
- Turnarounds.
- Companies just going public or just getting listed on an exchange.
- Companies breaking out of their roll range with better earnings, new products, et cetera.
- Traditional penny stocks with some reason (pressure) for the stock to go up.

What Wade Says Now:

Bottom Fishing Bear Market Plays:

We want to buy stocks in a metaphorical pressure cooker—having all the characteristics of a major gainer. In a bear market these turnarounds, coming out of bankruptcy, new start ups, et cetera, probably won't explode. But if the proper homework is done, if you get in early and stay diversified, then the ride should be okay. Again, not excellent, but better than most.

This may also be a good time to review the stocks. Bottom fishing stocks you purchased previously—say in a bull market. Do they have strength? Are they widely held, or not? Would a recession take the wind out of their sails? Or, are they strong, with new and better earnings? Are they up in a down market? In short, are they still a keeper? In a good market, use these to build income and use that income to buy quality stocks.

Buy Good Companies:

This strategy is just what it says. Good, well organized, well managed companies with good products are good investments. In any market.

Call Options:

A call option is the right to buy a specific stock. You buy call options when you think the stock is going up. This could be after a slam (serious down movement), on a roll, (when the stock is at the bottom of the roll range), or when a stock has good news, et cetera. In short, when you think the stock has pressure to move up, buy a call, ride it up, and sell. Since many stocks would go down in a bear market (just because it is a bear market and not because of any change in the stock) call options may be very profitable. Especially if purchased when the stocks are low. Yet, this can be very

Buy Good Companies Bear Market Plays:

What more is there to say? Buying good companies is always a good strategy (especially when they've just gone "on sale").

Call Options Bear Market Plays:

*Avoid call options on companies which have peaked. Watch earnings carefully. Look for serious slams ($10 to $13 dips) and be patient—wait for clear signs of strength. Read the "Dead Cat Bounce" section in **Stock Market Miracles**.*

Don't always go for doubles, take 20% to 40 % quick returns and look for more quick movers.
DON'T TRY TO CATCH A FALLING PIANO.

risky in a down-trending market.

DUCks:

Some of you have read elsewhere about DUCks—or Dipping Undervalued Calls. Usually occurring after a stock split, this is when a stock which has been climbing pulls back temporarily as investors take their profits. The company is solid and growing, but the stock dips 5-10% for no reason other than profit taking. Around our office, we have a word for this. We call it a "SALE." The price of the stock and also of the options, has just dropped below value. It is a perfect buy opportunity.

Hedging:

One use for options is a "hedge." A hedge is like an insurance policy. You hedge to limit your downside. Let's say you just spent $10,000 and purchased 100 shares of stock at $100 each. You think the stock is low (either the company is really profitable

DUCks Bear Market Plays:
Either in buying the stock, buying calls, or selling puts, we want the balance of buying power to be positive. In a down market we need to sell exceptional strength. Not every stock recovers right away. In a down market it may take months (instead of weeks) for a stock to become a super market buy.

or that the stock has gone down—hit a low). $10,000. That's a lot of money to have tied up. You have unlimited upside potential and all the time in the world because you actually own the stock. Your only risk is a dip in the price of the stock.

This is to let you know that during the five business days following the Wade Cook Wall Street Workshop, I averaged approximately $250 a day using only the covered calls technique I learned during the workshop. In addition, by working with a full-service broker, I was able to obtain 500 shares of a strong "takeover" stock for a possible 30-40% profit.

All things considered, I am confident I have started on a realistic course to financial independence. Thanks to all in Kent for their time and expertise. Wade was correct when he said the workshop is worth more than 10 times the tuition amount.

—Richard S. Kent, Washington

However, this can be a considerable risk. So, you hedge. You have two choices. 1.) You sell a Put option for near the price you spent on the stock. This way you gain the premium as insurance if the stock price goes down and stays down. 2.) You buy the short-term Puts at a comfortable strike price (out one to two months and then reevaluate the situation: company news, the stock price near the expiration date, et cetera) or further out puts below the strike price. They're cheaper and also give you more time. By looking at the company's chart you can determine how much you want to spend, how much time you want to buy, and how much risk you want to hedge.

Peaks and Slams:

Every day there are several stocks which close several dollars higher. They usually move higher on news. Sometimes, but very seldom, they do so for no reason whatsoever. The good news is usually about

Peaks and Slams Bear Market Plays:

A down market will look like a reverse range rider. We've used these for years so the strategy is the same. Buy on lows and sell on highs. Even if you're a little off the market, you should still be profitable. BE

Wade Cook's workshop . . . was a skeptical seminar for me to go to, even though I have invested in the stock market for several years. My first attempt at options was at the WSWS last week. I generated $3,256 in one day while at the workshop! Since then, in the next week, I made another $2,270. I am excited about the opportunity to be home with my children while I am making money for my husband's and my retirement. Thank you for teaching me a few formulas and giving me hands-on experience.
—Dawn—Poway, California

earnings—and if the earnings are great, the new high might be sustained, but if it's something other than earnings, i.e. a takeover, a merger, new product, stock split, etc., the news can play out very quickly.

As in the "Dead Cat Bounce" strategy, the Peak Strategy happens very quickly. You have to be ready to move not only on the purchase but also to sell. I usually know my exit (sell price) when I get involved. I believe we live in a very short-term society. We forget good news in about three days. It takes three months to forget bad news. This is only my conjecture, "the gospel according to Wade." I have no empirical evidence to back up the three day/three month statement, only a string of profitable trades using this as a guideline.

Rolling Options:
Options allow you to invest in the big stocks by proxy, using a small amount

CAREFUL, CHECK THE CHARTS.

Rolling Options Bear Market Plays:
This is one of the best "predictable" cash machines. Get good at look-

of money. Buy calls or sell puts when a stock is at its low range and then buy puts, or sell calls, when it peaks out and starts back down. This gives you a way to make money on both sides of the movement.

Rolling Stock:
There are certain stocks which trade within a certain range. Some brokers call this channeling. They move up to a high (resistance) and then to a low (support). Many stocks do this, but the ones I like (so I don't have a lot of cash tied up) are cheaper stocks—say in the $1 to $5 range. I find a stock which goes from $2 to $2.75. It doesn't seem like a lot of profit, but 75¢ on a $2 invest-

ing at charts. Check the momentum indicators (from your charting service or from your broker). Options are risky, so be careful. Make sure the stock, and hence the option, is heading in the desired direction. In a down market, consider buying a little more time—say out three to four months, instead of one to two months. USE THIS ONE ALWAYS, IN GOOD TIMES AND IN BAD TIMES.

Rolling Stock Bear Market Plays:
This strategy still creates predictable returns. Believe it or not, many stocks roll faster in down (or flat) markets. More people are watching the news. News makes stocks roll.
STICK TO THE RULES IN BOTH TYPES OF MARKETS.

ment in one to three or four months is not bad.

The three rules of rolling stocks are:

(1) You always know your exit before you go in the entrance.

(2) Don't get greedy—sell below the high for quicker and surer profits.

(3) Stick with the less expensive stocks—so you can buy more.

Selling Puts:

Obviously, any buy opportunity on a rising stock also presents a great opportunity to sell a Put. If the stock turns and rises, you keep the premium and that's it. Of course, you want to pick the stock near the bottom of the dip and sell the put for the very next expiration date. The strike price should be very near the stock price.

If you're wrong and the stock gets put to you (you may be required to buy it), you get it at a wholesale price. When you buy a ris-

Selling Puts Bear Market Plays:

Selling Puts is my favorite cash flow strategy. It's a cash flow generator and if you actually take the stock, do so at wholesale prices.

This is one strategy you should get good at. Watch the margin requirements. If you get the stock, sell calls on the next rebound. Don't wait too long. Remember, the formula is used, primarily to produce income. USE THIS STRATEGY BOTH BEFORE A DOWNTURN AND AS WE'RE COMING OUT OF A DOWN TURN.

ing stock (and one at a low price), you can sell later at a profit, sell calls, or just hold it. DUCks and selling puts really present a great opportunity to enhance your cash flow.

Short Selling:

Short selling allows you to borrow stock, sell it, and generate income. As the stock moves down, you purchase it, pay off the loan (borrowed stock) and pocket the difference. It's easier said than done.

Short Selling Bear Market Play:

In any down market the "shorts" come out of the woodwork. They are hoping for a continued down elevator. Consider the following:

1) *You can check the short sales on a particular stock. Your choice then is to join in the crowd (I don't) or wait it out and catch it on a bounce (I do).*
2) *Sometimes heavy short selling becomes a self-fulfilling prophecy. Be careful.*
3) *Put option volume is also a good indicator.*
4) *The bears on a particular stock can kill you, wait and beware.*

I'VE NEVER BEEN BIG INTO SHORT SELLING AND I'M NOT ABOUT TO START NOW.

Stock Splits:
My favorite method is to buy Call options on companies announcing a stock split. We get the best of both worlds, which synergistically really heats up the cash flow. There are many reasons why companies announce a stock split, or a stock for dividend.

There is a tendency, once a company does a stock split, for the stock to regain "lost ground." It may take a year or two or more, but think of that: If a $100 stock becomes two shares at $50 and you purchased it at that price, and one to two years later it is flirting with $100 again, you would double your money. What if, as a play, you purchased ten such stocks. One doesn't go anywhere; seven double in a year or so; one doubles in six months; and one doubles in a year and the stock splits again. Wow!

Stock Split Bear Market Play:
Announcement of stock splits are seriously curtailed in bear markets. Think of it. Most companies announce splits when the stock is high— after several quarters or even years of good earnings. But they may make an announcement to bolster the price of the stock in a bear market. If so, check earnings, debt, and growth projections. Make sure it's not just a PR play.

My formula is to play options on stock splits. In a down market, the announcement or actual split may be the news needed to get a quick bump out of the option. Don't put too much money into options as they are too risky.
USE THIS STRATEGY EXTENSIVELY BEFORE A DOWN TURN FOR INCOME AND PORTFOLIO ENHANCEMENT.

Tandem Plays:

There are many combinations, but my favorite is a combination of buying and selling Calls and buying and selling Puts. Here is how it works (See the chapter "Tandem Plays" in *Stock Market Miracles* for more on this):

When the stock is low, sell a Put and buy a Call—both strategies gain advantage with an increase in the stock price. You make money now selling the Put and you make more money later selling the Call option you purchased. When the stock is high, sell a call and buy a put. You make money on each as the stock moves down. This gives you four plays on a rolling stock with options.

Uncovered Calls:

This is called "going naked," in that you don't own the stock. You use this strategy when the stock is at

Tandem Plays Bear Market Plays:

If you maximize your returns and then put your money into good investments while the market is hot, you'll be so much better off. Use these "combo" strategies to load up. Then in a down turn, use them sparingly and wisely.
BUILD UP YOUR "CASH FLOW" ASSET BASE.

Uncovered Calls Bear Market Plays:

Think of this: If the stock is going down, selling calls and not having to deliver the stock is a pure cash genera-

the high part of its range. You sell the call—generating pure cash. You wait. As the stock moves down, your obligation to deliver (sell) the stock goes down and eventually disappears as the time expires. You make money with no investment. The risk is that if the stock goes up, you'll have to buy it at a higher price (offset by the cash you made for selling the call).

Writing Covered Calls:

Covered calls allow you to get consistently solid monthly returns of 14 to 34%. The idea behind this strategy is that you own the underlying stock, and don't mind keeping it. However, its price is fluctuating. So, you sell (write) a call option on your stock for whatever price you can get. Your position is "covered" because you own the stock. Even if

tor. Still, make sure you sell the calls when the stock is feeling some kind of strength.
THIS STRATEGY LETS YOU STAY A LITTLE GREEDY. BUT, don't sell Calls on stocks you think are going up; either buy the stock low (covered) and wait to sell the Call—getting a higher premium for the options and eventually selling (getting called out) at a higher price, or sell the Call when the stock is high—wait for a dip and then:
a) buy the stock or
b) buy back the option or
c) just let the option expire and keep the cash!

Writing Covered Calls Bear Market Play:

This is a good way to generate extra income on stocks you already own. If your stocks are down in price then sell slightly out of the money calls, so you'll more than likely keep the stock. Several months of incoming call premiums may be just the trick you need to make back any losses.

you sell the stock, you know you can buy it back at a lower price and repeat the strategy or just hold the stock.

You will probably get called out of less stocks (actually sell) in a down market.

Chapter 6

Bear Bottom

Very, very rarely, do I have an opportunity to get together with Team Wall Street—a collection of the speakers that are teaching the Wade Cook Wall Street Workshop, and people from my trading department, and research department. To get everybody together at one time in the Seattle area in a studio is really a thrill. The following are excerpts from a discussion we recently held with them.

Wade: Hi, this is Wade Cook. I'm here today to alleviate some fears that seem to occur whenever we have a robust market, and the bears come out of the woodwork. People start talking negatively and thinking negatively. I'd like you to join with me in discussing some of the things that we can do to watch out for, to avoid, to prepare for, and to profit from, any down turn in the current market. And I welcome all of you here. It's good to have you here because it's an opportunity for everybody to get together and discuss the market. You're all traveling all of the time and you meet all sorts of people and hear all sorts of ideas on the market. Because of that, you have many diverse viewpoints. I want to hear and discuss those, so, let's talk about a bear market. Where is all this talk coming from?

Keven: Well, I think you made the point already that whenever we have such a robust market as we've had for the last two, two and a half years, everybody always wants to focus on when it's going to end and how bad things are going to get.

Wade: Right.

Joel: Whenever you have something good going on, you're going to have somebody out there nay-saying it.

Wade: So they are bad-mouthing it? For what purpose?

Keven: Well, most of the investors have followed conventional wisdom, which says that we need to buy stock and hold it. That's where the money is made. And if there is no effort made to take the profit when it's there when the stock is high, then move out and wait for the best point to jump back in, those kinds of people will naturally fall prey to the market.

Wade: Okay, let's define a bear market before we go on. Let's ask somebody from our trading department. Pete, will you define what a bear market is.

Pete: Well, a bear market is anything from nine months to two years of a down turn in the market.

Wade: How much? What percentage of a down turn?

Pete: You can expect to see a 20 to 30% drop in the total equities in the DOW, or even in the Standard and Poors 500, or in the NASDAQ.

Wade: What if the market turns down in even a one or two month period of time? For example, the DOW goes from where it was last summer, $57,200 and then it's up to $7,000 now. Then it went from just under $6,000 clear back down to $5,400 dollars in a matter of days.

Joel: The market is always fluctuating, you're always going to have those little ups, those little downs, you're going to have a month when it slides off a few points. that doesn't mean it's a bear market. The downward trend has to be sustained.

Wade: You say you always have up and downs. Do you think that they are necessary?

Joel: Well, since the market's emotional, more than it is statistical, people tend to say, "Well, I've got my money, let's move out now," or, "Gee, I'm scared right now." You know, they have 1,000 emotions out there, so the market moves in bumps instead of moving smoothly.

Rich: I feel that's a valid point. Also, it works in the way of checks and balances on the system. The soft spots make people evaluate stocks and the market as a whole.

Wade: You're saying then that it's healthy for the market place to have a few soft spots?

Rich: I certainly believe that it is. If you get into the situation where you just have a true bull market, usually you're going to have the things that are going to be associated with that. Usually the rest of the economy is doing quite well. But, as that economy does well, as wages go up, you're going to have inflation going up, and you can have a tendency to have a runaway economy there. So you need to have these checks and balance systems in place, just to soften the market up every now and then to keep things in a good perspective.

Joel: You know, whether it's good for the market or not, it's good for me.

Rich: Definitely, there's money making opportunities there.

Wade: What causes a bear market? Not a crash, we can talk about crashes too, and a crash is obviously associated with a bear market, to a certain degree. But what causes a bear market?

Rich: There can be a number of factors. The main ones are bad earnings on companies, and higher inflation.

Wade: How are bad earnings, higher inflation, and other factors tied together?

Joel: The market pulls back because people pull their money out of it. And they take their money out of it because they're afraid. And so when you have high inflation, high interest rates, low earnings, they're afraid they're not going to continue to make money. That it's going to pull back, so it becomes a self-fulfilling prophecy.

Wade: Those are the three causes of a bear market: low earnings, high interest rates, and high inflation.

Keven: For at least the first down turn. From there it becomes protracted if the economy really does go south with the market or the interplay together. From that point, you have people who are making less money combined with the fear factor that they've just taken this big dip in the market. You have a reluctance to come back in with fresh money.

Wade: So you're saying that people may have gotten burned and it may take a shield for them to get back in.

Joel: Yeah. And people start looking for safer investments—CDs, bonds, et cetera—which higher inflation makes more attractive.

Wade: We don't need to belabor this point. Basically, in America, a bear market is caused by low corporate earnings, which are tied to or stem from high interest rates, or the thought, or the fear that there's going to be high interest rates.

Joel: And trade barriers and taxation. Those are two more factors.

Wade: Taxation?

Joel: Absolutely. A company that is spending all its profits on taxes isn't going to grow because they have no money to re-invest.

Wade: And if there are high individual taxes, people have less money to spend. All right, so what about trade barriers? We've got NAFTA, GATT, do those have any effect?

Joel: We've got so much of the world's population now that is interested in advancing their lifestyle and so forth, and the companies that are going to help them do that, many of them are located right here. So as companies expand internationally and continue to grow in phenomenal ways, like Coke and Caterpillar and Pepsi and McDonalds, the results will be phenomenal. We were thinking clear back in 1981 that McDonalds was topped out. Since then it's quintupled or 500 times its value as they move internationally, it's unreal.

Wade: I've decided that just one good way of playing the international market place is to buy stock in American companies that are expanding overseas.

Rich: As long as the world economy is doing well, a lot of these companies are getting a significant portion of their profits from overseas.

Joel: Right. All you have to do is do a little better homework, make sure that you're investing in the companies that are in the expanding markets.

Wade: I think that the rest of the world needs and/or wants so much of what we have. Especially when it comes to our biotech, our pharmaceuticals, our hi-tech computer hardware, software, et cetera. So, right now, does anybody see a bear market coming this year or next year?

Rich: No, if it does, it's going to be just a very temporary thing, maybe just like the one in June and July of last year. A temporary correction, just to try and slow down the overheating a bit. I feel that if that does happen, then it's going to turn around and take off and there's no telling where it might stop.

Wade: There are three bull markets for every one bear market. And by the way, just a quick note for anybody out there listening, if we've defined a bear market as a market that is down because of low corporate earnings, inflation, high taxes, high inflation rates, or high interest rates, then obviously the other side of that coin is that a bull market means good corporate earnings, relatively low taxes, relatively low inflation rates, and relatively low interest rates. So, that's the difference between the bear market and a bull market. In one you have rising stock prices, in the other you have falling stock prices. So my question was, do you see a bear market?

Joel: The reason why there are such widespread bear market predictions, I think, is the market has always had this general up trend, the broad 100, 200-year average of this general up trend. And then we saw in 1995 and right in the beginning of 1996, a sudden escalation of that. The market wasn't just going up gently, it suddenly screamed like a jet aircraft taking off. And so, when it slowed down in 1996 and into 1997 back to the gradual, gentle climb that it had done in 1991 and in 1985 and you know, all the way back, the people said, "Oh, no, it's topped out. It's going to fall." Well, what makes them think so?

Wade: Well, because they think the corporations, I guess, can't keep earning money. They can't keep expanding, they can't keep growing.

Joel: So they have no faith in the American system at all?

Wade: There's so much negativism out there and I get it everywhere I go. It's almost as if before I can teach people to make money, I have to deal with three or four negative people that show up just to be negative.

Rich: One thing I was going to say about the negativism on the economy is that it has a snowball effect because if enough people start saying that the economy is going to go bad, it almost eventually will, just because of all the negativism that comes in with that.

Wade: It becomes a self-fulfilling prophecy.

Rich: Exactly, a self-fulfilling prophecy, just like a snow-ball that just keeps rolling down the hill, it just keeps getting bigger and bigger, just keeps rolling faster. And even though the indicators may not be there, we will go into the bear market. Fortunately, if the indicators are still pretty positive there, it's going to be a very short-lived one.

Keven: The question is, where is the world going to go? Are we going to go that direction? Or are those third world countries going to come this direction?

Wade: They need what we have.

Pete: And look at democracy growing in the world. They obviously want what we have.

Wade: Let's get specific now. What do investors need to do now to get ready for or to avoid a bear market? Yes, at some time we are going to have a down turn, or a major dip in the market place, a 20%, a 30% dip in the market place. Whether it recovers in 6 months or a year and a half, sometimes the answer is so what? Let me just tell you what I'm thinking. And then you can comment on this. It doesn't make people money. And, it doesn't save them from financial disaster. All it does is use fear to keep investors from making money. I'm so tired of that stodgy old thinking. So, what do people do to get ready for a bear market?

Keven: The first comment I would make, Wade, is that you hit it right on the head. People talk about investing as they have practiced it for the last 80 or 100 years, it's all buy and hold. You buy a stock and you wait.

Wade: And you can't control what happens then.

Keven: There's no money in it. You are like a little tiny ship, tied to a big ship. And wherever the big ship goes, you go with it, whether you want to or not.

Wade: Right. So what are you saying? To not do that?

Keven: No, there's a time and a place for that, but it's certainly not a way to make money or get rich. You're going to ride over every wave, you're going to take every down turn along with the market instead of getting more profitable and waiting for another opportunity to get that thing on the low end.

Wade: That's a good point.

Joel: That philosophy, the buy and hold, is actually what you should be doing at the end of a bear market. That's where that plays in. People who have that mentality are thinking we're always at the end of a bear market. I was thinking that there are three things that we can do to deal with a bear market. 1.) We need to play the market at hand. You can't go through life trying to play something that doesn't exist. 2.) We need education. We need to know what to do, when and if. We need to become familiar with all of the different kinds of markets, the different kinds of stocks, different kinds of plays, and the different strategies. 3.) We need a cash reserve. If we, in fact, do go into a bear market, then that cash that we are holding is going to enable us to buy some really top-quality companies while they are on "sale."

Rich: But Joel brought up the underlying thing to this whole thing, you need to have the knowledge. To have that knowledge, to get the education, to have this know-how to be able to deal with these types of factors in the market is the key essence.

Wade: To know when to get in?

Rich: To know when to get in and more importantly, know when to get out. Because the emphasis is on selling.

Wade: All right, you said three, I'm going to add number four. Diversify. I don't want to have anybody coming to my seminars that does not learn the underlying principle of diversification. It's the "not having all your eggs in one basket." So, for example, you might have $10,000 but don't put $10,000 into one stock. Or one option. Put $10,000 into ten different stocks at $1,000 each, right? Take a gamble on ten of them, instead of one. Buy ten good stocks and do all of them. All right, but I want to spend just a second and not talk about diversification of stocks. What about diversification of formulas? Diversification of methods or ways of making money?

Joel: Absolutely, it's critical. People think of diversification, and they think that means to buy different stocks, so they do. But all the stocks are in the transportation industry. I mean, we have to diversify by sector, by company, by strategy, by method, by everything.

Wade: Okay, let's just go through a quick list here. And let's isolate any of these that are pre-bear market in nature. And when I say pre-bear market, I mean getting ready for a bear market, trying to build up and make as much money as you possibly can. So that when there is that little bit of a 10%, 20%, 30% dip, that your $10,000 has grown to $200,000, so that a 20% dip takes you down to $160,000. But while everybody else is boo-hooing and back with their $10,000 saying, "See, I sat this one out, I didn't get caught in the bear market." But you're going to, and anybody listening right now is going to, have their $10,000 sitting there still at $160,000, after this thing is over.

Rolling Stock. When a stock rolls between a certain range, it rolls up and rolls down repeatedly, it is a rolling stock.

Writing Covered Calls. Buying stock and selling options on it to generate income, and hopefully getting some capital gains along the way, as a way of generating income so that you have more profits then to buy more stock.

Bottom Fishing. Finding IPO's, turnarounds, other bankrupt companies that are coming out of bankruptcy, other companies that have the highest likelihood of bouncing back or going back up very quickly.

Selling Puts. You agree to buy stock at a certain price and you get paid for that agreement. You literally put yourself out saying, "I'm willing to buy this stock at this price," and you're hoping the stock goes up and you may not have to buy it, but even if you do, you get paid for the obligation that you took on that.

Stock Splits. Pure investing in companies that are doing stock splits, by buying the stocks, or by buying options. Let's talk about options in general. An option strategy, buying the right to buy a stock or to sell a stock that you think is going up and not buying the stock itself. Just a pure option, or pure proxy play. Now what do all of these have to do with pre-bear market mentality?

Pete: That's really easy, because it puts you in a short-term cash flow strategy. You can be in and you can be out of the market before the bear hits.

Wade: So you're saying that a lot of people out there need a short-term strategy?

Pete: Oh, absolutely. I mean, even in a bull market you need a short-term strategy.

Wade: But what you guys have been saying all along is opposite from what everybody's teaching. What every stockbroker, every analyst, every company, every company on Wall Street is teaching is buy and hold.

Pete: Well not everyone. There's Wade Cook.

Wade: But, I'm serious, I feel so sorry for people that all they do is call their stockbrokers and it's buy this stock and don't sell it. And they never hear, "Hey, buy the stock at $3 and when it gets to $5, sell it." They don't hear that, they never hear that.

Rich: And they are leaving so much money on the table that way.

Joel: There are brokers that are teaching that, because, after all, where did we learn? So somebody out there is teaching this stuff, it's just not very many. And most people don't hear it. And the folks that are teaching it, do it for a couple three years, and then they are wealthy enough to retire in Tahiti, and then who's teaching it?

Wade: Right.

Keven: I heard a really interesting comment last week in an Anaheim workshop, and this gentleman approached us and said, "I have a friend who is in a major brokerage in San Francisco and I won't name the brokerage. But my brother and I have a string of restaurants and we have a fairly large sum that we wanted to invest and we approached this broker and we asked him what he thought of Wade Cook's strategies and he said, 'well I don't know who this Wade Cook guy is but he's doing stuff that only about 5% of us even know how to do, and it's the upper 5%.' "

Wade: But Wade Cook is a cab driver that happened to get on a platform, he got a microphone. And so he's got a best-selling book. So Wade Cook is doing that, but when my book first came out, I was being criticized by everybody.

Joel: Well, it's only the upper-echelon brokers that know what's going on.

Wade: Now I've got brokers, by the way, that'll only let their students trade if they go through our training or read our books. My book has been a best-seller, the *Wall Street Money Machine*, now my new book, *Stock Market Miracles*, is the same thing. It's got so many broker-related strategies, but, *Wall Street Money Machine* has been kept a best-seller by stockbrokers buying 10, 15, 20 books at a time for all their customers. But there's still other stockbrokers that haven't read it that criticize it.

Keven: The back end of that story is that they gave him a book, Wade.

Wade: They gave that stockbroker a book?

Keven: Yes.

Wade: Cool.

Keven: Now he knows who you are.

Joel: It's awfully easy to be down on what you're not up on. That's cliche but it works.

Wade: All right, now, I want to deal with this word "diversify" for a second. I just gave several strategies. To you, what is the difference between a formula, a strategy, a method. I guess "buy and hold" is a formula, but that's the only one, right? I mean, when you do that you have to live by that. I guess what I'm after is making money, using the stock market to make money, to turn it into a business.

Keven: There are so many tools that it is incredible. We talk a lot about options at our workshop and we might want to discuss this in greater detail, but buying and selling of options gives you so much leverage that you can turn a small movement in the market, or the stock, particular stock , into a huge gain, and in my mind, that gives you the knife that you can use to cut the rope between your little boat and this big ship that may be heading for the reef. So you go wherever you need to go.

Rich: But we're using formulas here. These formulas are something that have been proven, they have stood the test of time. They have worked before, they are working now, they'll keep on working in the future, no matter whether we're in a bull market, bear market, whatever. These are proven formulas.

Wade: We need to wrap this up, and I appreciate you being here. Everyone listening, just because we might, and I repeat, might, go into a bear market does not mean that you have to go into a bear market. You don't have to have a bear market mentality. There are always options, there are always opportunities, there are always ways of making money, in good markets and in bad markets. I encourage you to be careful to whom you are listening. To come and join with our Team Wall Street, get on our WIN, our computer bulletin board service, listen to our home study courses, watch our video courses, we are the number one, the premier financial educators in America. I often say, "We've got the best seminar in the country." But then I take a look around, and there's nobody in second place. There's nobody else even there. So when I say, we're the best, we're number one, there's nobody in second place. We're the only one that's there. So I encourage you, right now, to pick up your phone, do not delay, it's going to cost some of you 10, 20, 30, $40,000 a month to wait to take the Wall Street Workshop. It's 800-872-7411, this has been Wade Cook with Rich Simmons, Joel Black, Pete O'Brien, and Keven Hart, hoping for you the best future. We wish you well and hope that you prosper and if there's anything that our staff can do to help you make more money and keep more of what you are making, then that is what the Wade Cook Seminars are all about. Again, call 1-800-872-7411. Thank you for listening.

Chapter 7

Bear Tracks

Knowledge is of two kinds. We know a subject ourselves, or we know where we can find information upon it
—*Samuel Johnson*

There are two types of formats for determining stock values—both attempt to ascertain the movement of a stock's price. One is fundamental analysis and the other is technical analysis. I have weighted my decisions in favor of fundamental analysis, mostly out of personal bias. It just makes so much more sense to me. I have done well following, examining, and looking at the fundamental strengths (debt load, earnings per share, earnings strength, yield, and book value) of a particular stock, and thereby the economy as a whole or in sectors.

I have also done well with certain angles of technical analysis. It works well for locking of patterns (break outs, DUCks, gaps, et cetera) for quick plays. I have not, however, done well playing the information from technical analysis for long-term play. They have been so wrong lately.

This is possibly where most bears incubate, or at least hibernate. Computer modules are just not that accurate. Imagine software people getting together to figure out where the DOW will be in six months or a year. Their predictions, backed up by their software programs, have to be scrutinized carefully. Just a few well-placed "Techs" can devastate a stock, or give credibility to one which should be ignored—yes, it has great technicals, according to point-and-figure charting, but lousy fundamentals.

The Four Hated Words:

Every time the market defies estimation, the cry is, "This time is different!" It's almost cliche. Am I to believe we're in uncharted territory? Yes, there are some aspects that are the same this time around, but we are where no market has been.

Prices are a tad high, but not so for most companies. People are paying high multiples for some stocks, but 8 to 12 Price/Earnings abound. There are some great bargains. There is no IPO fever, even though the volume is picking up. Earnings may have peaked in 1995, but they may be poised, or "plateaued," for a new surge. Inflation is down. The Fed is tinkering, but ever so slowly—trying to avoid both an increase in inflation and a recession. Investor confidence is relatively high. This could be bearish, but several other indicators point to increases in production, exports, and growth.

In a bull market, an "over bought" condition typically lasts longer, while a "oversold" condition ends very quickly. The reverse is true in a bear market.
—Alan R. Shaw

Yes, this could be seen as bearish, but there is just too much good happening to say this incredible bull cannot go on a little further. Baby boomers are getting older, many segments of the economy are truly solid. I'm going to ride the bull a bit longer.

Even many of these bearish technicians are turning optimistic. One says we'll be at DOW 8250 this year. Some predict a 12,000 DOW by the year 2001 or 2002. One thought explains much of this. Some think that excessive bullishness is actually bearish. I don't know about that, but when the market crossed

7,000, the proportion of bulls to bears (in market newsletters) was less than 50%. Everyone keeps thinking, or saying, "This has got to end." I don't view this as overly bullish. Most bears, especially those in the closet, come out every time there is a run-up in stocks.

Obviously, the market's not going straight up. It never has, and it never will. There are many peaks and valleys along the way. Look at this chart of the DJIA. We see similar charts when we look at specific companies. The DOW is a range rider. The market as a whole is a "Rolling Stock."

The American opportunity of ours gives everyone a great opportunity if we only seize it with both hands.
—Al Capone

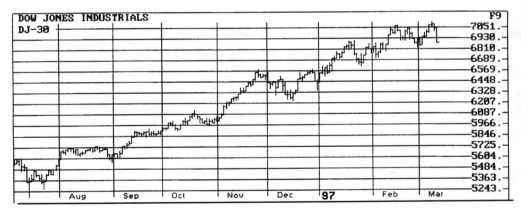

Okay, let's get past the philosophical and get down to how to play a bear market. Here are a few strategies to keep your mental life jackets above water:

Read everything you can get your hands on. Really study. Pay attention to signs which foretell market direc-

The first rule is not to lose. The second rule is not to forget the first rule.
—Warren Buffett

tion. Is it still going lower, or is it turning around? Just because stocks are in a bear market does not mean that you have to be in a bear market. There are always stocks which go up. Bear markets do not mean an end to volatility. Most of my strategies have their basis and strength in volatile stocks:

Write covered calls for income.

Play range riders, and now reverse range riders.

Look for value and "dip"—trying opportunities.

Attend a Wade Cook Seminar/Workshop. We have been, and will remain, on the cutting edge. Already copycats abound, like that big-tooth phony from San Diego, but they are just copycats. Wade Cook Seminars will have workshops, symposiums, and other forums. We won't stop helping people learn how to retire rich.

Be more careful. In an up market, everything works (except buying puts). In a down market, one has to be more selective.

Learn how to use charting services.

Technical analysis becomes much more important. If you don't want to learn these strategies yourself, then tap into services and newsletters which use them, but more importantly, make recommendations, or at least point out stocks/options which fit.

Base decisions on conflicting opinions. Do a lot of research, ponder, then pounce. Buy good companies.

Follow earnings. Companies with great earnings will be the last to go down and the first to recover.

Stick with the tried and true. Big company stocks are not always the best place to be, especially if earnings growth has slowed, and/or the price/earnings ratio is high. "Tried and true" means bread and butter industries with proven records.

Follow closely (closer than in a bull market) news announcements. Watch for trends. When times are bad, everyone is watching the news. Stick to the formulas that work, don't let temporary setbacks stop you from trading.

Don't panic. Waiting it out in today's high-paced economics is probably time-honored advice you should employ—either in a bear market or on serious correction.

Imagination is more important than knowledge.
—Albert Einstein

Initial Public Offerings (IPO's) may not be the best place to be. Incidentally, IPO's slow down to famine levels during bear markets. If an IPO is on an existing company with market share, low debt, and a history of profits, its IPO could do quite well. I avoid the highly speculative companies.

Diversify stocks. Build a portfolio of solid, proven winners. See **Stock Market Miracles** for a major writing on this.

Diversify mutual funds. Not only pick a mutual fund which best reflects your needs, but own a variety of mutual funds. Many funds get hit hardest when there is a downturn. Why? Many have/own the same stocks. They all go in the entrance one at a time but then rush for a crowded exit when there is a panic. They own so much of certain stocks, when they unload major positions, it can seriously drive the price down.

Diversify strategies.   I've written about my eleven stock market strategies in other chapters and other books. *Wall Street Money Machine* and *Stock Market Miracles* teach these formulas, and at the Wall Street Workshop. In times of negativism, dips and recession, bear markets lighten up on the more aggressive plop-like options. Still, study the fundamentals and play stocks and options in a reverse or downward-trending way. Be wise, be diversified.

Avoid Thirteen.   Just kidding, but do avoid mismatched comparisons. It seems everyone has their buddy chain, their rationale (when the GOP wins, the 2nd year of the 2nd term of the President, the 10:00 am to 11:00 am time period on Thursdays, etc.). I read these because they're amusing, but be leery of this nonsensical advice. There are exceptions to every rule, including these observations. Besides, I get tired of changing the width of my ties to influence the markets.

The quality of a person's life is in direct proportion to their commitment to excellence, regardless of their chosen field of endeavor.
—Vince Lombardi

Hang around people who are achieving in companies—bet on the jockey. In life, be careful when you listen to advice. Get on WIN (Wealth Information Network) and use it for all it's worth.

Stay focused on how to generate income when times get bad. Back up a little and take a hard look, make small forays (with stocks, but especially with options) into the market plan. Monitor your results, learn the new rides and keep going.

Be quicker at cutting losses than in a bull market. I dedicated a whole section of a chapter in **Stock Market Miracles** to getting out of investments -- especially cou-

> *Don't be scared to take big steps—*
> *you can't cross a chasm in*
> *two small jumps.*
> —David Lloyd George

pled with the "why" of getting in. Simply put, how can you know when to sell unless you know why you bought? Now to the point here:

Long Term: If your strategy was to invest in a great company for the long term, than you should plan to live with the vicissitudes of the stock. Selling should take place after the story line has changed, either in your own life or the life of the company.

Short Term: If your strategy is as a cash-flow generator, a quick in and out, then monitor your purchase more carefully. Put in sell orders when you purchase, and if it doesn't behave quickly, then get out and move on.

It either works or it doesn't work. As Yoda says in *The Empire Strikes Back*, "There is no try, there is only do."

The people that love you the most will put you down the most. Sad, but true. Get them knowledgeable. An uninformed mind is negative when confronted with new, (wild to them) strategies. Be careful to whom you go for advice.

Chapter 8

Bear Traps

*When you reach for the stars,
you may not get one,
but you won't come up with a handful of mud either.*
—Leo Burnett

Follow these ten steps and you are guaranteed to fail in the stock market. True poverty and frustration will be yours.

1. Don't diversify. Keep all your eggs in one basket. Keep life simple. Bet it all on red. Also, don't learn functional methods to increase your cash flow. Variety is not the spice of life. Anyway, you don't need more income, so stick with the "buy one stock and hang on" theory.

2. Don't read anything. There's so much weird stuff in the world, so what's the use? Don't seek out a diversity of opinions. There's too much information available—our minds are on information overload already. So, don't explore. Don't be concerned with the economic "signs of the times."

3. Look at past performance of stocks and invest in companies affected poorly by a recession or by negative conditions. Look for the worst, buy into the worst, be the worst.

4. Don't worry about income. You won't need more cash flow later so don't sell anything—including options (to generate income) on stocks you already own.

5. Don't worry about the quality of your stockbroker. Anyone will do. If they say or do negative things, follow them. If they bad mouth education, seminars, books, then follow their advice. If they want to be your only link to the world of profits, then go for it. If they're not "up" on it, they'll be "down" on it. (Note: The author believes a good stockbroker can make you a fortune, but you've got to find and train him/her to be good). And don't think of having two stockbrokers. Who would want a second opinion, or someone else finding good deals?

6. Make sure you ask the opinion of everyone at work and church—especially those making $35,000 or less a year. They're tuned in to what's going on. Also, seek out people who know someone who lost their shirt in _____ (gold, stocks, business, real estate). You fill in the blank. Avoid successful people.

7. Pay no attention to fundamentals (analysis). Ignore earnings—especially companies with increasing earnings. A company's debt is of no concern, so don't worry about it. Who cares about dividends and yields?

8. Play every insider tip you have. News from people "in the know" is very hard to come by. Shoot the wad on it. Who cares what they (whoever leaked the news, or made it up) have to gain by it.

> *Beware of inside information . . . all inside information.*
> *—Jesse Livermore*

9. Ignore temporary dips, or pull back. Remember, opportunity only knocks once. For you, it was when you were 23, so why look for more chances to make money now?

10. Don't educate yourself. It's a waste. Avoid the Wall Street Workshop at all costs. Who wants to

learn how to double your money every two and a half to four months? Who wants to be retired in ten months? And anyway, who wants to be in a 40% tax bracket? Stay home and stay poor—let's not upset the apple cart.

In a bear market,
what's the difference between a stockbroker
and a pigeon?
The pigeon can still make a deposit
on a BMW!

Whoever said, "You pay for education once, you continually pay for ignorance," just didn't know what they were talking about.

Chapter 9

Bear-ing Teeth

Obstacles are those frightening things you see when you take your eyes off the goal.
—Hannah More

A common and integral part of my gold seminars is to encourage people to stay on the gold standard—at least to a certain extent. Just because America has gone off the gold standard does not mean that we have to. A part of our assets should be in gold.

Now in my stock market seminars, I encourage people not to go into a bear market mentality. Just because we enter a bear market does not mean all is lost. We can fight back. We can prepare. We can sit it out. Our choices are varied and have profound consequences.

I'll divide this section into two. The first part will be dealing with a bear market, the second dealing with stocks that act like they're in a bear market, even though we're in a bull market.

Down Market Stocks:
The theme of this section is the opposite in character. Just because we enter a bear market does not mean that every stock goes down—or goes down dramatically. Some are recession-proof and some even fare very well.

I'll make three general comments about finding good stocks in down markets:

1) News articles, but more specifically, magazine articles, are loaded with information about companies which fare well, or have fared well, in down markets. This genre of news proliferates during bad times. Major firms, and financial news updates, go searching for values, bargain stocks, stocks which fared well in previous downturns, stocks which rebounded quickly, and stocks with good upward potential. I remember these well in 1990 and 1991. Then again, in 1994. I thought, "what?" They're starting again now. Even though times are good, a lot of the talk is bad. I can't, and won't, list these stocks here. By the time the information is needed, the list would have changed. Don't worry, these sources are everywhere, and well becoming more widespread if we enter a bear market.

Evil news rides post, while good news waits.
—John Milton

2) There are a few firms which analyze stocks. Some over analyze. Many stocks actually buck the trend of a downturn. These stocks are said to be "negative beta down" by the "techies." Let me explain. The beta of a stock is a measuring tool to see the volatility of a stock, or the likelihood of price changes, as measured against the Standard & Poors 500. The Standard & Poors 500 shows: 1. If a stock has a beta of 1.2, it is said to be .2 or 20% more volatile than the S&P. A beta of 2 would be a high flying, very volatile stock with a huge 2x increase compared to the norm. A negative beta, say .8, is 20% less volatile the norm of 1. The model can get more sophisticated. What if the market goes down and the stock has a positive beta? It is a stock which rises when the S&P goes down. A negative beta means the stock price increases, the down

means a down market. The analysis of stocks which fit this scenario could use several filters to finally elect stock in certain fields, or with certain P/E, or debt loads. However, I believe this information is valuable, if one is looking for stocks with good potential during down markets. Your stockbroker should be able to find reports on these companies. We could list several here but, once again, by the time you read this, the effectiveness of this would have changed.

It's not difficult to find this information. We put these on WIN when we find them (call 1-800-872-7411 to find out about our computer bulletin board service).

Fortune is like the market, where many times, if you can stay a little, the price will fall.
—Francis Bacon

3) Good charting services can help you trade stock performances, measure momentum or buying power. You should subscribe to one for current information.

Up Market Stocks:
In a bull market, many stocks do poorly. Some for no apparent reason whatsoever. Like the comments I've made about a series of events leading up to a crash, a correction, or bear market, is a phenomenon and the same happens with individual stocks. Big dips (and big surges) just happen. Maybe because of program buying or selling. Maybe bad news (buying out the short sellers). Maybe competition. Sometimes the events are explainable, sometimes they're not. I went looking for stocks which recently had a 20% decrease (sometime more than six months to twelve months ago). Look at how they've performed. I've made comments where I thought they were appropriate. Remember, these down or "bear market" stocks occurred in a bull market.

There are two major points I'd like to make with this next part.

No rule is so general which admits not some exception.
—Robert Burton

1) In up and down markets there are exceptions to the rule, or in other words, stocks which underperform or outperform the norm. It is finding these odd-balls and either ignoring them or figuring out how to play them which can make us money.

2) There are specific formulas, or methods, which can be employed to make money in any markets. In down markets (actually, this usually means flat market after a serious decrease in value) there are companies which excel. Yes, it's tough to buck the trend but well managed companies not only do better, but they attract investors like a powerful magnet. The law of supply and demand takes hold and you have buyers choosing a few good stocks, driving the price up.

If you've followed the formulas given elsewhere in this book and throughout my other books, you would have been near the first to enter the picture, and in line to make substantial profits once the increase takes effect.

In up markets there are still companies doing poorly. Let's look at the chart of several of these companies with running commentary on how to play them. Please see Range Riders and Reverse Range Riders in *Wall Street Money Machine* and in *Stock Market Miracles*. If you can learn how to play these now, think how much better off you'll be when the whole market acts like one of these stocks.

```
APPLE COMPUTER INC   o*                                              F2
AAPL                                                              49.04
                                                                 46.85
                                                                 44.66
                                                                 42.47
                                                                 40.29
                                                                 38.10
                                                                 35.91
                                                                 33.72
                                                                 31.54
                                                                 29.35
                                                                 27.16
                                                                 24.97
                                                                 22.79
                                                                 20.60
                                                                 18.41
                                                                 16.22
   AMJ      JAS      OND   96    AMJ     JAS     OND    97
```

Apple Computer, a widely held stock, and one which is frequently in the news, is our first candidate. In the middle of 1996 the stock was near $50. In the spring of 1997 it was around $17. Look at the peaks and valleys. Too many opportunities for profits to list here. Look at the gap up in the '96 July/August, and the December 96/January 97 gap down. Gaps are a tremendous play. Once the stock breaks out (up) or gaps down, the trend continues for the next few months (until more news comes out). This is more than a 60% decline from 1996 to 1997. With a few 20% one-to-one-and-a-half month down periods. (Note: Study range riders in *Wall Street Money Machine*, and peaks and slams in *Stock Market Miracles*.)

From $33 to $22 in seconds. Now it's a rolling stock. Might this stock recover? Let me answer a question with a question. Isn't this a good time to check the fundamentals? Also, wouldn't you like to know why it fell in the first place—and then continued falling? Consider buying $10 or $12.50 strike price call options when it dips

below $10. Buy them out at least two months to give it
time to roll up—then get out with a 50¢ to 75¢ profit. Ten
contracts would generate a profit of $500 to $750, with an
estimated investment of $1,000. Also, consider selling
puts when it's low and buying puts when it's high. Could
be a good covered call stock.

Look at the two sharp down turns, (A) and (B). This
stock fell from $46.78 to $25 in 15 months. The Dow Jones
Industrial Average was having a great year. Look at the
number of times it fought to go back up. Has it estab-
lished a new bottom? This might be a good one to check.
If you read this book later than the spring of '97, check it
out. Is it rolling? Is it turning around? Are the options
expensive or cheap?

This stock used to be part of the Standard & Poors 500.
In December of '96 it was taken off—replaced by Conseco

We go to the movies to be entertained,
not to see rape, ransacking, pillage, and looting.
We can get all that in the stock market.
—*Kennedy Gammage*

(CNC). Look at both of their charts. Find the bottom of this one. When the change was made, I loaded up on Conseco.

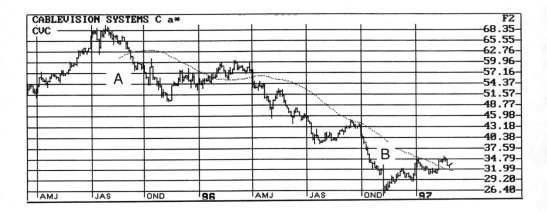

Look at the streakiness of this fall: from $34 to $8 in five months. It looks like it's coming out of the doldrums—but not by much. Also note the serious dip in July of 1996, when almost all stocks dipped.

Chapter 10

Bear With Me

The following is a modified transcription of a heated panel discussion and interview between the host of Your Money Matters, *John Childers, and Cheryle Hamilton, and Wade Cook, author of numerous books, including* **Wall Street Money Machine** *and* **Stock Market Miracles***. There is a powerful interaction going on. It's hard, it's fast and in quick-step time the listener, now you the reader, gets a useful earful of easy-to-implement ways to make money in any market, up or down.*

This is John Childers from *Your Money Matters* and we have as our guest today Mr. Wade Cook, author of **Wall Street Money Machine** and **Real Estate Money Machine**. You seem to have several books out here Wade and they all seem to be selling so well. Can you just tell our audience why your books are selling? In fact, even before you answer that, I want to know particularly about this book the **Wall Street Money Machine**. It seem like everyone who uses your methods is making money in the stock market. Why is everybody buying your book?

Wade: Well, I don't know if everybody is making money, and if they are making money, it may be that they're making money in terms of inflation—as in increasing stock value, but when you say "making money" to me—and that's exactly what my book is about—is that it helps people who are not so much interested in a stock or a mutual fund. I'm interested in helping people to get in, get out, and make some cash, and when I say cash, I mean actual cash. Send it to the house, get a check, use that cash to buy other investments, use that cash to buy some real estate, support your family, go buy a new set of roller skates for your kids, I mean that's the kind of cash I'm talking about. So my book puts the emphasis on building up income.

John: Well, that seems to be a little bit different from what my broker is telling me. My broker is saying that if I just trust in him I should buy something and hold on to it and you're telling me something a little bit contrary to that.

Wade: Maybe that's okay for some people, and maybe that's okay for you. I don't ever give any recommendations. However, most people who really want to quit their job or quit their businesses just don't have the income to do so. The one thing they need to replace is income and by taking, say $5,000 or $10,000, and put it into IBM stock, they're out of control. You know, whether the stock goes up or down, whether the company pays a dividend or not, they're out of control. If the market is good and if inflation keeps in check and if interest rates stay low, then maybe their stock will do well, but it still doesn't provide any income. Maybe there will be a small dividend paid, but the amount necessary to live on would not be there.

Cheryle: Wade, there is a lot of comment out in the financial world right now about the market going into a bear market. Your strategies are about cash flow and you're going about it in a bull market. How is this going to work in a bear market?

Wade: Well, obviously we can all take advantage of a bull market. Anybody can. It's hard to go wrong in a bull market. I mean you can buy almost any stock out there and it's going to go up in value. It's like swimming downstream with the fish. You're just going in the same direction—it's easy. It becomes tough when you change around and swim upstream. My point is, you play the market at hand. Whatever is there right now, that's the game that is in town, and that's the game you play.

Right now we're in the midst of a bull market and there is a lot of talk about a bear market. In a bear market, you just have to be more careful. You say, "What do I do?" Well, you put the emphasis on strategies. For example, my rolling stock strategy or range rider strategy. In a bear market, these will change and become what we call a reverse range rider. Throughout my books, the **Wall Street Money Machine**, **Stock Market Miracles,** and at my live Wall Street Workshops, we teach bear market strategies all the time: to diversify—to make sure that you don't have all your eggs in one basket. If you're doing options, for example, you buy some short term options and some long term options. You have in your portfolio certain stocks that you're in and out of. Some are like guerrilla warfare, you get in, you get out, and you make a lot of money. You also have other blue chip type stocks that you hold.

There's even a process called the "negative beta down." You can call your stockbrokers and say, "I want a list of stocks that go up when the market goes down." Now, a beta is a measurement of the volatility of a stock. Negative means the stock is going up. But when you say down, that means a down market, like a bear market is down. So negative beta down means that you can find stocks that go up when the market goes down. And there's a whole bunch of them that do it. We have lists of stocks that go up when there is a bear market. So, knowledge is the key: knowing what to do in any marketplace.

Cheryle: So, you're saying the same strategies you teach in your books and your seminars will provide the basis for playing a bear market and a bull market?

Wade: No, not necessarily. Some of my bull market strategies should be reversed. You do the opposite of my strategies. You would take certain strategies and literally play the opposite side of it. For example, I'm really big into buying call options on companies. In a bear market, you would buy puts. In a bull market, you can just buy anything, so the opposite strategy is, you don't just buy anything. You're very selective in a bear market. You do a lot more research. You get a lot more into the technical figures like point and figure charting and other things like that, and find stockbrokers who are really good at technical analysis. The profits are going to be minimized unless you do extra homework. If you want a lot of profits, then you have to be more careful in a bear market than you are in a bull market.

John: Well it sounds to me that what you're teaching is different than what my broker has been telling me to do.

Wade: What has your broker been saying about a bear market?

John: He tells me to buy and hold. What's bothering me, and I'm sure it's bothering our audience out there, is the fact that if you buy and hold and if the bear market takes over, we're going to be buying and holding as it's going down in value.

Wade: Right, and who wants to do that?

John: It looks like you've got some different strategies here, and what I want to know is, will your strategies protect me if things turn bad?

Wade: Well, if it changes, it's not going to change that dramatically. But there's no reason to believe a bear market is going to devastate anybody's portfolio. That has not been the case in the last 70 or 80 years. The only thing that affected the stock market, even at the time of the crash of 1929, was not so much the crash as it was stupid government policy. The Smoot Hawley Tariff Act put up incredible trade barriers all around the world. It drove our economy into such a long-lasting recession, and about the only thing that bailed it out of that recession was the Second World War. In 1987, for example, the stock market crashed. It literally crashed 30%. That crash, by the way, was, in terms of percentage and dollar amounts, a lot more serious then the stock market crash of 1929, but it lasted under a year. For example, if you had had $100,000 invested in 1987 and the stock market went down 30%, that means your investments went down to $70,000. But just a little under 13 months later, it was back up to $120,000.

Now, what if you had learned one of my strategies which would have had you buying on serious dips like that. You would have jumped in at $70,000 and ridden it back up to $120,000. You would have made a huge profit. Nevertheless, even if your existing portfolio had gone down, you still would not have lost. One of the things about bear market strategies is to not panic. Don't start selling everything when everybody else is selling. You should buy when other people are selling and you should sell when other people are buying. When a stock makes a really high run up and everybody is catching it on the momentum, say the stock has gone from $100 to

$120, if you happen to own that stock and everybody starts jumping in at the peak, the high value of that stock or price of that stock is not going to be sustained. That's when you should be selling. When other people are buying, that's when you should be doing the opposite. Don't have this herd mentality.

Back to 1987, if there's a huge crash, not only in the market place but in particular stocks, that is the time to get in. Now, I'm not saying we're going to have a bear market or not. I'm saying we're not going to have a bear market *now*. Not now. Not this year, probably not next year, not with interest rates being in check and a Federal Reserve just bent on making sure there's no inflation. This means they're going to keep a tight cap on interest rates and they'll raise them just a little bit now and then to keep inflation down. If inflation is down and if the interest rates are down, and companies are doing well, earning a lot of money, then it does not point to a bear market. Now that's the point.

You know, we've never had anything like the serious dip of 1987 in the history of the stock market. Did that affect the companies? It may have affected a person's portfolio, but they're still driving down the street seeing Coca-Cola delivery trucks at 7-Eleven. Okay, so Coca-Cola stock went down $10, but the price of their products didn't go down $10. There's a world of difference between getting caught up in the negative sentiment in the stock market, but then you've got to walk outside and say, "Hey, Ford is still selling cars. General Motors is still making cars. Microsoft is expanding overseas."

People say, "Well this stock should be down. The stock should have taken this dip." And so the everyday market place, the everyday running of America still goes on whether the stocks are up 100 points one day or down 100 points the next day.

What we've got to learn is how to take advantage of the volatility. When a stock goes down $9 in one day, from $80 to $71, we jump on it and ride it back to $80. That's what we need to learn how to do, and that's what I teach in all my other books and now in my seminars: showing people how to look for opportunities, and there are opportunities everywhere. Opportunity does not knock once, it knocks every day. And there are deals to be made every day.

John: I'm kind of confused on an issue here. If you were giving us a list of companies we should invest in, I could understand why they were selling like crazy. But you're telling us you don't give advice about which companies to buy and yet you're books are selling and you can't keep them in the bookstores. Why?

Wade: Because I don't give recommendations on certain companies. In my books, I do mention certain companies but only for illustrative purposes. I use particular companies as examples to show people a certain scenario of what might happen. We may put in charts to show patterns. What I am into is formulas. I'll give several of them. Rolling stock—where you find a stock that trades between a certain range. It goes from $2 up to $3 and back down. Another formula is range-riders where a stock will go from $70 up to $77, then back to $72, then up to $80. It's on a climb, say from $70 up to $100, but it's not a straight shot. So it goes from $70 up to $77 back off to $72. The next time it goes up to $80, but it goes back down to $73, three or four weeks later. And every time it makes a dip back down, you ascertain the bottom, which is not tough to do, and then you buy it right there, or buy options on it right there. And then when it hits, it's now high, that's when you sell it. It peaks out and it comes right back down. That's called Range Riders. That's the name I made up for this movement.

How about writing covered calls, or buying stocks that are on serious dips? I mean talk about bear market mentality. My whole covered call scenario is talking about buying stocks on dips and then selling the options on those stocks and generating income. Another strategy is to sell puts. Selling puts is where you agree to buy stock at a certain price and you sell puts when you think the stock is going to go up. So when a stock is low, you buy a call option and you sell a put option. When a stock is high, you sell a call option and you buy a put option. Now I've outlined this in **Stock Market Miracles** under tandem plays, you know doing two plays while it goes up and then two plays while it comes down. Now you have stock brokers who say, "Well, you can make money in any market," I say, "Hey, not only can you make money in any market, you can make money twice as much when the stock is going up and twice as much when the stock is going down, if you know how to play them."

Cheryle: This incredible enthusiasm and optimism in the face of what we're getting out there is exciting for the people who are listening, but you know we're all affected by the media, and hearing all of these things, how do we avoid all this negativism?

Wade: That's a great question. You've got to keep things in perspective. Let me give you an example. This morning before we did this interview, I was reading an article. Now listen to what it said, then I'll turn this interview around and ask for your response. It said this: when they started doing the Dow Jones Industrial Average, basically from the beginning the stock market was formed, it took 88 years for the Dow Jones Industrial Average to get to the 1,000 level. Now, the Dow Jones Industrial Average is a blending of thirty different companies on a weighted average of their stock. It took 88 years to get to 1,000, but it took from November of 1996 until February of 1997 for it to go from 6,000 to 7,000. It went up 1,000 points in four months. Did you catch that? 1,000 points in four months. It went 1,000 points in 88 years, and now, it went 1,000 points in four months and people are saying, "That's too fast—1,000 points in four months." So when some read this they say, "Wow, we're ripe for a crash because it's gone up too fast." What's your response? What do you think? What this article was trying to say was, "Watch out everyone. We've got a crash coming."

John: Well, my response would be, I need to know more about the market, learn why these things are about to happen and what I should do with my money.

Wade: Are you scared by hearing that though?

John: Well, a little bit.

Wade: OK. What do you think?

Cheryle: Actually, it makes me more curious. I think I would want to get more involved in trying to figure out really how can I profit myself. How can I prepare my portfolio so I can be crash proof, so to speak.

Wade: OK, I think that was the intent of the article. That's what they wanted to do. Make people think they need to have a better mix of stocks, or get out of the market. But not me. You see, I look at the 88 years for it to go from zero to 1,000. Well, look at the percentage. To go from 6,000 points up to 7,000 points, what's that? That's about a 17% growth rate. So 17% of 6,000 would be 1,000. There's a 17% difference between 6,000 and 7,000. What is the percent difference between zero and 1,000?

Cheryle: 1,000%.

Wade: See the point? So it naturally took 88 years. Now if they went back and they said it took two years for it to go from zero to 100 then that would make more sense, right. So they use 88 years, but it had to go clear from zero. The percentage rate of growth to get from zero to 1,000 is absolutely so much more remarkable. It is much more phenomenal than in four months going from 6,000 to 7,000. But when you put what people are saying and what the market is doing in perspective you say, "This is not that bad of a deal." You know, it's not that great of a rate of return.

Cheryle: No. You're looking at 15-17%.

Wade: The last couple of years it's been on 20%.

Cheryle: It's up a little better than average but it's not phenomenally different.

Wade: That's right. That's the point, to answer your question. You've got to keep it in perspective; is this really that high, or outlandish, or weird? Your question was how do you deal with all the negativism. You've got to look at the intent of that statement being made. So, I look down at the end of the article and sure enough there was a financial planner in some city, (they didn't give his phone number) but you see what I'm saying. What's their intent? Their intent is to sell a newsletter. Their intent is to pick you up as a new investor so you'll spend all of your money with them, so they can make commissions off of all your investments. You see, and to answer your question about my seminars, I get nothing out of what people do. I don't want their money. I don't invest their money. I don't make recommendations on their money. I want to teach strategies, and the people keep all their own profits. I'll show them how to keep everything in perspective. I'll show them how to work the formulas. I'll show them how to make the money. They get to keep all of their profits and that's the big difference between me and everyone else.

John: I'd like to change the subject here, Wade. It sounds like you know a lot about your stock market strategies. You've written extensively about them. I'm sure you've made a lot of money, but for our listening audience, the average, hard working person, what does this all mean to them? What does it mean to those who are just getting started?

Wade: Let me give you several things people can do to get them on the road to wealth right now. 1) Currently, we are in the middle of a bull market. Play the market at hand. Don't get caught up in the pessimism that there might be a bear market or that you should bullet proof yourself as much as possible. You should be buying your investment in entities that pay no taxes. For example, bombproof your investments in legal entities like Nevada Corporations, Living Trusts, Pension Plans, etc. In fact, I have an entity structuring tape cassette seminar that I'll send anyone for free. Just call 1-800-872-7411. It's called the Entity Structuring tape.

2) You ought to be buying stocks and also trying to diversify your portfolio, not only into real estate or other business interests, but into stocks that are diversified—

even blue chip stocks that hold up well in bad times. I have a subpart to number two. The problem with what I just said is that a lot of people listening right now would like to do more, not only buy more, but buy better investments. They don't have the cash to do it. If they scrape together 10,000 bucks and put it into Coca-Cola or IBM, their money is tied up. What I've tried to show people at my seminars is a way to use the stock market itself as a business. Buy and sell, buy and sell, get in, get out, make a profit. Then take some of your profits and keep it moving. Take some and buy these better investments, these blue chip stocks.

Another part of number two would be to buy investments that hold up well. Use "Negative Beta Down" to find investments that are recession proof. There are a lot of companies which do well in bad times. They just are not affected by recessions, some thrive in recessionary times. You definitely want to have some of those in your portfolio.

3) You want to buy stocks that are widely traded. You want to avoid little no name stocks. So in a bear market you want to have stocks that everybody else wants to own. In real estate, we used to teach people to get in the way of progress. You know, buy a piece of ground where the mall is going. Buy and try to guess where the freeways are going to go.

In the stock market the way you get in the way of progress is to invest in companies that all these big mutual funds will want to invest in. Think about it. They've got to invest. For example, one place to invest would be into the Dow Jones Industrial stocks themselves, or into any of the 500 stocks in the S & P 500. Why? Because huge mutual funds have billions of dollars, trillions of dollars of assets that have to invest in just those stocks. Period, that's it.

For example, a couple months before this interview one of the companies got dropped out of the S & P 500. They added Conseco, the ticker symbol CNC. The stock went up $5-$6 within a couple of weeks. Why? Because many of these mutual funds have to buy that stock. They had to get rid of their stock in the company that was dropped from the 500 and buy Conseco stock. They have to own it. They're index funds. They own all the stocks in a particular index. You get in the way of progress by owning stocks that everybody else wants to (or needs to) own.

4) You want to make sure that you find a good stock broker. Somebody who can really educate you. Somebody who is a little bullish on the marketplace, or is at least bullish on education and knowledge. Somebody who has a good computer system and who can track stocks well for you; someone who can get research reports for you, tracking services and things like that. It basically comes down to not only what you know, but who you know.

5) And the last point is to get educated. I mean, I don't care what anybody is doing, they need to come out to my seminars or someone's seminars. If they don't come to mine, they've got to go somewhere but, you know, the somewhere else doesn't exist. I want to say we have the best Wall Street Workshop in the whole country and I turn and look around and there's nobody else in second place. We have the only seminar that teaches people on a hands on, experiential basis how to do deals and work formulas, so they are involved. So that they start making money.

We get people so excited about making money, indeed actually making money that they'll take a portfolio of $10,000 and turn it into $30,000 in a matter of months. Triple their money. Now, think this one through. If they now have $30,000 and there's a stock market crash, are they better off? Let me make a quick point about stock market crashes. I don't see a bear market around the corner anywhere near us right now. But could there be a stock market crash? Yes. A 10%, 20%, or 30% dip? Yes. We keep having little corrections. We need little breathers. These corrections are really nice. Down 90 points in one day and then it climbs back up over the next week. It's not bad, but a consolidation time. A time for some to take their profits. A time to recover. But look at the strength (the breadth and depth) in the current market. We have a new thing, something they didn't have in 1929 called Program Trading. For example, a lot of funds which own a certain stock which hits $90, the computer triggers a sale. All of a sudden, orders are flying. When a whole bunch of the same funds own the same stock and start selling them, bam, all of a sudden the stock goes down to $80 almost overnight. And that's called a stock market crash.

Also two points on that. Number one, obviously we want to avoid stocks which every one owns and ones likely to be dumped. We want to be diversified. Number two, we want to take advantage of those. So always have some money in cash. Always. That's one of the things we teach at our seminars. Have some cash ready to take advantage of opportunities. Don't spend all your money right now. Keep some in reserve so you can jump in on these really serious dips in the market place.

John: I don't mean to put you on the spot, but I guess maybe I do mean to because I think I owe it to our listeners to ask you this. These people that are coming to your seminars, are they really making money?

Wade: They really are making money. They are buying new cars. They're putting down payments on houses. We had one guy that we just heard of on the Internet the other day who started with $20,000. In about six and a half or seven months, he was over $300,000. A guy came with $30,000 and made over $700,000 in five months. I can't even read all the letters anymore, all the testimonials. We show people how to make money. We tell them, we show them, and then we have them actually do it. Now many people make money right during the class. I mean the cost of the seminar is made back, sometimes even more. 30-40% of the people make back the cost of the seminar right in the class.

But the point is about making money. After the class is over they just keep it going. They learn a formula, it's repetition, it's duplication, and they just turn it into a little machine. One person may come and really like rolling stock. Another person comes and really likes covered calls. By the way, most people really like covered calls. That's the number one strategy that people use after the course—writing covered calls. Other people love selling puts and other range rider strategies. They pick the one that they like. They get to be an expert in that one, and then they use it repetitiously.

So my point is, you gotta make hay while the bull climbs. Play the market at hand. It's climbing right now. You take somebody that has $10,000 and they run it up to $100,000 in even six months or nine months or a year, and then if there's a 10% or 20% decline, what do they have? And what would you rather have? A 10% decline on $100,000? OK, so you're only worth $90,000. So big deal. You started with $10,000 a year ago and now you're worth $90,000. Even if you're down to $70,000, you're still a lot better off. You've got to keep everything in perspective and not get caught up in all the negativism that's out there.

Cheryle: You're making it sound like it's just as exciting to play a bear market as it would be to play a bull market.

Wade: It would be. Because the strategies, even though they're different, will be pretty much the same, although some will be reversed. You have to be a lot more careful and use the technicals. I'm sure that both of you have had times in your life when you were a lot more flush than you might be right now, or maybe much worse. You know, you lost your job or something and you go to the grocery, actually you shop at different grocery stores, right, and you shop better. It's the same thing in the stock market. When you've got a little bit of money and your money has to go a long way and when there's a bit of a down market, you're just more careful on how you shop. When everything is going well, when you've got a full box of soap to do your laundry, you use any amount you want. But when there's only one little scoop left in the bottom you start rationing—using half scoops. You're just more careful. You adjust.

Cheryle: So this sounds like making lemonade out of lemons.

Wade: It is exactly that. Again, though, there are some people who are always going to be negative. And I'm asking everyone who is listening to this interview right now to not worry about that so much. Use this negativism that's in the marketplace for your benefit. It's kind of like keeping a check on runaway inflation. It keeps a check on the market.

There's a lot of program trading that goes on. There's a lot of profit taking that goes on. A stock goes from $60 up to $90 and people say, "I'm happy here." If it hits $100 then a lot of people sell it. Well, all that selling activity drives the stock back down to $90. That's when we can jump in and take advantage of it, when it hits a new bottom. We need the bears with us. We need people out there talking negative. I don't want them to go away. I just want the people listening right now to keep it in perspective and to realize what they're after. A lot of people get so negative—they think a stock is going to go down so they short sell the stock. Then you see them bad mouthing the stock because they want the price of the stock to fall. That's why I've never been big on short selling. It changes your mental attitude. I don't want to be constantly thinking about things going down.

We as Americans, in this rugged individualistic country, have a driving need to grow and to thrive. So do companies. The drive takes on a life of its own. Many companies want to grow, to expand, to do better, to build in quality. As long as that drive exists in America, (and who says that's ever going to go away) I want to invest here.

Remember a couple years ago when everybody said, "Well American productivity is down compared to the Japanese and the Germans." Hogwash! We came back and beat their butts. We are so much better in our productive hours right now than anybody. We are the country that everybody is coming to. We are the country where all the money is coming. We may have slumps from time to time, but this is the country that has this incredible attitude. So this is where we need to be and we don't need to be ashamed or afraid. I guess the point I'm trying to make is this: just because the stock market might go into a bear market phase, does not mean that anybody listening to this, any of our students, has to be in a bear market mentality. And let me say one more thing. Keep this all in perspective.

I know I've said this in all of my seminars. Realize that the average bull market lasts three to five years. The average bear market lasts about nine months. The last one was only six months in 1990. Compare three to five years and nine months. Think of the comparison there. And there are three bull markets for every one bear market. So to what should anybody listening right now be gearing their strategies. So what if there's a bear market? Go on vacation for six months or nine months. Then come back and play the next bull market. They should not get caught up in negative mentality. In all of my books and at my seminars I say to keep everything in perspective. Don't get wrapped up in the negativism.

Cheryle: You know, you have just provided the confidence I need now to start working with these strategies. Often times I'm hearing, "That's fine, but what happens if I get into trouble? How do I work with it? I don't feel like I can afford this." You're telling me now that I have the ability to work with these strategies in a way that allows me to continue on. It's not going to impede me. I'm not going to lose money just because the economy decides to take a turn.

Wade: You may lose money on any particular deal, but you won't lose money overall. Not if you keep a long term perspective and you keep using your profits in your short term deals to buy (long term) better stocks. And even if you have a stock that you bought at $60, like a Coca-Cola, and it runs up to $90 or $100 and then goes back to $80, your $60 is still $80. What if you started with $10,000 and in a year or two you built it up to $200,000, and now your money is in better stocks. They then have gone from $200,000 to $250,000. All right? Then there's a 30% drop back down to $175,000. So what? You see, you've got to keep it in perspective. Nobody wants to see those kinds of drops but you shouldn't be panicking just because there's a <u>dip</u> in the marketplace or a crash—mini crash or a maxi crash. You should not panic. That's one of the mental things you have to keep up, there's always tomorrow. Hey, that sounds like a Broadway show.

John: Well, I'm excited! I know Cheryle is excited and our audience is probably excited. What do we do from here? What steps do we take starting right now?

Wade: You get in the market place. You open up your brokerage account. Hopefully you'll come to one of my seminars and get educated. Read my books. Get other books. Go to every book store and buy every book on the stock market you can. Keep it in perspective. Remember we need the bears so you read a little about bear market strategies, but start doing something. Start now. Take $500, take $1,000 and start doing something. You're going to learn by experience (that's what we do at the Wall Street Workshops is teach people by experience), but the most important thing right now is to start doing something. Just get $500 or $1,000 or $5,000 or $10,000 invested and get that money moving and turning and making profits to buy more and better investments for tomorrow.

John: Thank you very much Mr. Cook.

Chapter 11

Grin and Bear It

Man's mind, once stretched by a new idea,
never regains its original dimensions.
—Oliver Wendell Holmes

Cacophonous sounds emanating everywhere. You'd think that the bear market was already upon us. However, many people who have been listening to these emanations from seemingly knowledgeable sources have missed out on some of the most tremendous gains in stock market history.

The market crash of 1987, a nearly 30% drop, has become a new benchmark for a serious correction or major dip in the market place. That dip, that correction, was a lot more than the stock market crash of 1929, both in terms of percentages and in terms of dollar amount. I remember seeing numerous people on TV wailing and moaning about the loss of their pension money. I'm also sure that their financial planners and other financial professionals were telling them to go ahead and sell because it may even go down more. While it may be true in some cases that cutting your losses is good advice, it sure was not true in this case. Any person with any money sense at all would have realized that this was a buying opportunity, and not a time to sell.

One of the answers to the question we receive about knowing when to sell is to only sell when you would not buy. Could not this strategy be used in reverse—you should not sell when you would consider buying? It's the opposite, but pretty much the opposite side of the same coin. When there are swings in the market place and particularly peaks and valleys in any particular stock's climb, that points to a formula for buying on weakness. You would look to buy on dips in the stock price or when the whole market price is down.

When the prices are high they want to buy; When the prices are low they let them go.
—Ian Notley

It is my firm contention that we are not soon headed into a bear market. I know that this is good news for a lot of people and while it is not news to me, it is my best educated guess after looking at several stock market and economic scenarios. I do not contend that I am an expert as an economist in the market place in general. I am an earnest investor, a dedicated observer, a cash flow practitioner, and a concerned citizen.

This concern has led me to the belief that countless tens of thousands, possibly millions, of people are getting bad advice and have sat out one of the largest stock market rallies in the history of mankind. Why? Because it seems like negativism prevails everywhere. I say this tongue in cheek because to me optimism is the key to success. Do not bet on pessimistic statements, do not gamble on negative people, and surely do not invest your mental energy in gutter dwelling comments. There are so many opportunities to make money both in up markets and in down markets. We have to explored some of those possibilities in this short book and hopefully show the readers many ways to not only make money but then to mitigate any losses on any dips in the market.

My books, **Wall Street Money Machine**, and now **Stock Market Miracles** have been so popular because they give people hope and actual strategies which create actual cash flow. I want you to read a letter I received from a surgeon.

Dear Wade:

I wish to thank you for your wonderful contributions. I'm writing not only to express my gratefulness, but to share an experience I had about two weeks ago that has more to do with the human experience than directly with financial success. On a Friday your tape arrived and I was wondering when I was going to find the time to listen to it. At 1:00 a.m. that very next morning there was an emergency call for me (I am a practicing vascular surgeon of 20 years). And I was groggily dreading another sleep-deprived weekend. On the way to the hospital, I heard most of the new tape, and was amazed at the transformation of how I felt. By now I was fully awake, alert, refreshed, and eagerly anticipating what lay in store.

I now realize what took place. You gave me something very important that early morning. That something is HOPE. Hope, one of our most powerful emotions, is the essence of motivation, and is priceless. Hope means different things to different people, but to me it means the promise of a less demanding profes-

sional life, of a life actually being with my family, of being able to retire from medicine rather than being retired by it, of financial security in essence. Hope is the future!

I profoundly thank you for rekindling that spirit that is within us all. Moreover, you are providing the power through which hope is operative. That power is EDUCATION, that engine we need to move us forward. Education is inestimable and irredeemable. You have that unique ability to make complex matters seem readily comprehensible. As a surgical educator I know what a rare gift this is. Again, I thank you for sharing your special talents.

Sincerely,
J.K., M.D.
Oregon

I had no idea that my methods would have such a dramatic impact in peoples' lives. This is a beautiful letter. I do not get many as articulate and eloquent as this, but I do get hundreds of letters and testimonials every week from people who have been through my seminars and who are now living better lives.

Let me tell you a story about what happened to one of our instructors. The other night he had a visitor in his home and when the man found out that he did financial seminars he berated the stock market in many ways. He brought out all the negative ideas about risk. He paraphrased (but thought he was quoting) many financial gurus. Obviously he was taking bits and pieces of different scenarios and different comments and putting them together into the most awful future scenario he could muster. This person was so wedded in negativism that our instructor had a really hard time getting a word in edgewise, let alone being able to rationalize with this man.

Finally, when the man was almost out of steam and after having said several of his sentences redundantly, our instructor was able to get a word in. And here was a simple scenario that he gave. "I am making about 40% a year on my money. (Actually he's doing better than that, but negative people surely don't want to hear good news.) Over the last two years, my $100,000 has grown from $100,000 to $140,00 to over $180,000. So, if there is a 10 to 20% dip in the market place and I go back to $150,000, am I not a lot better off to invest while the market is good, to run up my profits to the highest level that I possibly can, and then if there ever is a downturn in the market I'll be much better off than having my money sit this one out? Won't I be much better off than if I have my money in a bank account?" Finally the man had no answer.

If the models are telling you to sell, sell, sell, but only buyers are out there, don't be a jerk. Buy!
—William Silber

I'm going to propose the same situation here: What will it be like if you do not participate in this stock market rally? Take what profits you can, play the economy, play the market for all that it is worth. Use cash flow strategies to build up your income, but then take this income and build up your asset base. And don't panic.

It is to this last statement that I'd like to address some remarks. Let's go back again to 1987. I do not have the exact quotes in front of me. I do remember, however, reading many, many stories about people and what happened to them after the stock market crash of 1987. This was such a serious crash and it made such major headlines and it seems like the news media was out after anybody they could find whose face they could put on the television screen or on radio news interviews that would bad mouth and bring out all the negative aspects of the stock market. The comments that I read a little over a year later—I think it said thirteen months later—said the market was up about 120% from where it was the year before.

Let me put this in perspective. If you had $100,000 invested, in 1987 in the crash it would have gone down about 30%. You would be down to $70,000. A little over one year later that $70,000 of net worth, your original $100,000, was up around $120,000. Think of this, just for waiting it out you would have been rewarded handsomely. I'm certain that most people did this—even though there was negative talk all over television. Most people didn't run out and sell all their stocks. Now I know that there was a lot of selling going on but a lot of that was program trading, which, by the way, triggered the biggest dip in the 1987 crash. Now think this one through. If you would not have panicked and would have even started buying when everybody else was selling, you'd be so much better off.

If you don't profit from your mistakes, someone else will.
—Yale Hirsch

Imagine waiting for another crash of this nature, of this degree, and jumping in and buying those stocks at $70,000 and riding them up to the $120,000. Now you would not just have a $20,000 profit on your original

$100,000 investment, you'd have a $50,000 profit on your $70,000 investment. These are the kinds of returns that we're really looking for. Use serious dips in any particular stock or in the market place in general as a buying opportunity. Then, here is a simple technique (as taught in the Wall Street Workshop) using good solid cash flow formulas and techniques to build up your income. Get and remain profitable by using these cash flow strategies and then buy good solid stocks and mutual funds. Buy them with profits. See the related chapter in **Stock Market Miracles** and learn how to get free rides. Just invest. Use the strategies I personally tested to make you cash flow rich.

Keep away from people who try to belittle your ambitions. Small people always do that, but the really great make you feel that you, too, can become great.
—Mark Twain

Appendix 1
Why WIN?

One way to keep up your optimism is to hang out with Wade Cook and his Team Wall Street every day. While you obviously can't be with this power-packed group of men and women physically, they have created a computer bulletin board service where you can not only see what they are doing, and why, but you can talk with other people who are using Wade Cook's strategies to become rich also. This incredible service is called WIN, or Wealth Information Network. To sign up and learn more about other opportunities that are available to you, call Wade Cook Seminars, Inc. at 1-800-872-7411.

Following are very brief examples of what Wade Cook and Team Wall Street have shared on WIN over the course of the last year. Most of the information put on WIN is real examples of real trades and the results. These clips are solely to show what Wade Cook and the Team Wall Street have been saying.

Before we list some of what's been said, let's hear what one stockbroker had to say:

Dear Wade:
*I figured the small investment for your book, **Wall Street Money Machine**, would be worth the risk. I was so impressed that I subscribed to the WIN bulletin board service. Now my life has changed forever!*

An example of one of my first investments was in Sybase Inc. (SYBS). I purchased 300 shares on October 2, 1996, and then sold 3 covered call contracts on them and was called out on October 18, 1996. My return was 23.73% in 16 days or a 534% annualized return.

Wade, you are a Godsend. Thank you for providing the tools and information to really make money and have more time for church and family.
Sincerely,
Chuck L.

May 1996:

If any of you are thinking of getting information on Berkshire Hathaway (BRK) you sure should. At least to follow what is going on. I think I have reported on this once before, but I will go ahead and tell you once again. In all of the advertisements and announcements I have been getting in the mail from my stockbrokers and Charles Schwab, they are trying to solicit business for an IPO that is coming out on the Class B shares of Berkshire Hathaway (BRK). I do not know the ticker symbol of the new class of stock, but May 8 will be a big day for the stock market.

It is interesting though, because they have not mentioned the amount of share for the IPO. They did say they will make enough stock available to take care of demand. It seems to me that the stock may not have a run up. I wonder if this is what they did with Lucent (LU) a couple of weeks ago? When that stock came out at $31, literally millions of shares sold at $31. Usually, when an IPO comes out at $20, it shoots up to $38 or $0 and then backs off a little. It is a typical deal, based on supply and demand—the sentiment in the market and what is driving the price of the stock up. But, when Berkshire

Hathaway (BRK) makes an announcement that they are going to meet the demand and they have enough stock available to raise a lot of money, does this mean that they are going to sell all the shares at a set price? Let's talk about that set price and then I will try to come back and answer the previous question.

Good morning everyone. This could be a very interesting day in the market. This is one of those crazy days where everybody thinks the market will be slammed, and it probably will. The unemployment reports are out, and they are not bad, actually they are quite good. More jobs have been created, but unemployment went up 2/10 of 1% up to 5.6%. But, because it is so good and the economy is so good, they are figuring the Federal Reserve will step in and raise interest rates which will drive the bond market down and the stock market will follow. Go figure this kind of reasoning. It happens almost every quarter, but it is totally crazy. In light of that, I am going to do a couple of things.

This should be a very interesting day to watch the market. Keep your eye on it—there may be a lot of opportunities. Remember, a lot of times news plays out in an hour or two.

July 1996:
Good morning everyone. It is a few minutes before the stock market opens. I have a feeling that this is going to be a slow week, with July 4th this week, so I am not gambling on too many robust plays. With the lack of volume in the market, there will probably be a lot less up movement. After speaking with several of my brokers, I think there is some consensus that the market will be having a summer lull right now. I don't know the cause

of this, but the first time in a long time the market is feeling weak. So, I guess the word is just caution and I would not gamble on any big plays. Obviously, there are always winners among the losers and even with the market going down there are still some good plays that can be made. But, overall, one of the lessons I have learned is not to fight the trend. Do not swim upstream when everybody else is swimming downstream.

I will be very cautious in the next few weeks and try to buy options on weakness and take advantage of the negativism in the market. Here's an example: Coca Cola (KO) is around $48 to $49 and it looks to have had a nice steady climb since it did its split (2 shares at $40), and at the long term prospects for the company looks favorable and the market backs off and this stocks drops down to around $44 or $45 and seems to find a new bottom at this range, I would jump back in and buy some October or November calls. Buying them far enough out and waiting for a market turn around. This is the kind of play that I will be looking for. There could be individual slams amidst a sector that is going up and there can also be a lot of losers. I will just get more selective now, and take on a little bear market strategy of looking for the diamonds in the hay stack. I will be more selective and a lot more careful. That's probably not bad advice for anytime in the market place, but more so right now. If the market does soften, the options that I have been buying may not materialize with profits as quickly as before.

This should be a short day. It will be interesting to watch and see if the market comes back. The individual stocks that are getting slammed could come bouncing back. It looks like the economic news is good, but the market goes down. This really does not make any sense.

Hello once again. I just got a call from by stockbroker on Astea International (ATEA). I purchased 1000 shares the other day. Remember, this was the one that fell $14 in one day. It went down from $22 to $8. I was waiting for a dead cat bounce. I think I got it. It is back up to around $9-1/2. I could sell out and make a small profit. I bought it at $8-3/8 and I could sell right now at $9-1/2 or I could wait a little bit longer. Since the whole market is down right now, it may come up a bit more. I told my stockbroker to try to get out at a $2 profit. I will just have to wait and see what happens.

Good morning everyone. The market went down about 4 points and then it went right back up. It was up 5 points just a minute ago. Right now, it looks like there is not going to be the big selloff that was predicted over the weekend. A lot of people estimated it was going to go down another 50 points. Some of the stocks are down and some are up. It is just a normal market right now.

Good morning everyone. The market has just opened and there are several plays already. If the market comes back, which it has a likelihood to do after having a bad week, there could be some nice plays this week.

Conceso (CNC) is down around the $37 range which looks to be the bottom part of its trading range. The August $35 calls were trading around $2-7/8. The November $35 calls were trading around $3-7/8, but there was not a lot of trading going on with those options. I told my broker to purchase a few contracts if the pricing is still the same when the market opens. The November $40 calls closed Friday at $1-9/16, so I may purchase some of those also.

I am heading in to play basketball, but I have my broker checking on stocks that were slammed last week to see if there are any worth jumping in on. I will check on those as soon as I finish playing basketball.

Good morning everyone. This has been a most unusual two days. With the market zigzagging like it was yesterday, it was not for the faint of heart at all. I will make a few comments on the market in general, and again I am no sage on this sort of thing. A lot of the volatility is in the high-tech arena and it seems to be that there is nothing in these high-tech companies including IBM (IBM), Microsoft (MSFT) and Hewlett-Packard (HWP), in the actual day-to-day operations or the profit-making earnings that they are actually accomplishing, that would justify such wild swings in their stock. Just keep that in mind. The companies seem to be solid, they are expanding, growing and they have good earnings. To see their stock up and down like it has been, there is no justification for it except for just a fickle market place and a lot of investor sentiment. Keep everything in perspective and learn how to take advantage of the big swings. I did that yesterday with several stocks and it was very profitable.

For example, if you read my comments yesterday, I was sad that I had a GTC order on buying Avon (AVP) July $40 calls at $2-1/4, and I should have just put in a day order only, because I forgot about this order. When the order was hit, within in minutes they dropped to $1-1/2. I could have lost money, in that they are July calls which expires on Friday. I considered this money gone and chalked it up to a mistake that I played on a GTC order instead of a day order, or in that I did not cancel the GTC order. Anyway, I had my stockbroker put in an order to sell them at $2-1/2, which he did. With the volatility of the market, I was expecting to lose money, but I ended up making money.

Checking on several other slams, there are quite a few of them out there including Xerox (XRX). Xerox (XRX) is trading around $47-1/8 and it has done a 3:1 stock split. It was trading around $51 or $52. The August $50 calls are trading around 13/16 which is little bit tight, but the October $50 calls are trading around $1-7/16 x $1-11/16, so I placed my order for ten contracts on those. I told my broker as soon as that order hits, to place a sell order at $3-1/2.

Let's talk about Safeguard Scientific (SFE) first of all. I was doing the "dead cat bounce" strategy on this one yesterday. I bought the August $55 calls for $6-1/8 and I bought the November $60 calls for $7-3/8. This is a stock split company, but it has gone way down. I got hit big time the last few days so we bought it on the bounce. It did bounce back up yesterday. This morning, I got out of the August $55 calls at $9-1/2. I got out of the November $60 calls at $9-5/8. I am adding up the profits—they are around $14,000 to $16,000.

Appendix 2

Why Wade?

Why Wade? It's a valid question. Why should you spend your hard-earned money and even harder-to-find time learning Wade Cook's methods and strategies? Well, for one, he only preaches what he has practiced and practiced and practiced and practiced. In other words, what he knows will work time and time again. Also, his strategies are safe—or, at least, as safe as any strategy can be. He works hard to insure that every safety net possible is built into the strategy. What is the proof of this? How do you know that this is true? This is how: following are three different proof of returns. No hype, no hiding, just the cold hard numbers for every deal he's done for the three weeks before this book went to press. After you've seen his results and are ready to start implementing his strategies, call 1-800-872-7411, and go to your local book store and pick up *Wall Street Money Machine* and *Stock Market Miracles*.

TICKER	COMPANY	REASON	BUY DATE	QTY	POSITION	PRICE	TOTAL	SELL DATE	PRICE	TOTAL IN	GAIN/LOSS	%	DAYS	ANN %
WX	WESTINGHOUSE		20-Feb	10	APR 17.50	1 3/16	$ 1,187.50	6-Mar	2 1/4	$ 2,250.00	$ 1,062.50	89%	14	2,333%
KM	K-MART		14-Jan	1000	STOCK	11	$ 11,000.00	5-Mar	13 1/8	$ 13,125.00	$ 2,125.00	19%	50	141%
DD	DUPONT	SPLT ANNCD	3-Mar	10	JUL 110	6	$ 6,000.00	3-Mar	7	$ 7,000.00	$ 1,000.00	17%	1	6,083%
	NORTH FORK BANCORP		25-Feb	10	MAY 40	2 11/16	$ 2,687.00	25-Feb	3 1/4	$ 3,250.00	$ 563.00	21%	1	7,648%
IMPX	IMP INC.		8-Jan	2000	STOCK	2 3/4	$ 5,500.00	6-Mar	2 15/32	$ 4,937.60	$ (562.40)	-10%	57	-65%
HTCH	HUTCHINSON TECH	3:1 2/11	20-Jan	300	STOCK	30 3/4	$ 9,225.00	25-Feb	36 1/2	$ 10,950.00	$ 1,725.00	19%	36	190%
WX	WESTINGHOUSE		21-Feb	10	JUL 17.50	1 3/4	$ 1,750.00	4-Mar	2 1/2	$ 2,500.00	$ 750.00	43%	11	1,422%
DD	DUPONT	SPLT ANNCD	3-Mar	10	JUL 110	6	$ 6,000.00	3-Mar	6 7/8	$ 6,875.00	$ 875.00	15%	1	5,323%
BQR	QUICK & REILLY	SPLT ANNCD	18-Feb	5	APR 35	5 1/2	$ 2,750.00	19-Feb	6	$ 3,000.00	$ 250.00	9%	1	3,318%
BQR	QUICK & REILLY	SPLT ANNCD	18-Feb	10	APR 40	2 1/4	$ 2,250.00	19-Feb	3	$ 3,000.00	$ 750.00	33%	1	12,167%
STT	STATE STREET	SPLT ANNCD	20-Feb	10	MAR 85	2 3/8	$ 2,375.00	20-Feb	3 1/2	$ 3,500.00	$ 1,125.00	47%	1	17,289%
SHBZ	SHOWBIZ PIZZA	SPLT PLAY	22-Apr	150	STOCK	14 1/2	$ 2,175.00	25-Feb	20 3/4	$ 3,112.50	$ 937.50	43%	300	52%
U	US AIR		17-Oct	1000	STOCK	16 1/4	$ 16,250.00	25-Feb	20	$ 20,000.00	$ 3,750.00	23%	131	64%
NIB	NEW IBERIA BANCORP		22-Aug	300	STOCK	14 1/6	$ 4,250.19	25-Feb	20 7/8	$ 6,262.50	$ 2,012.31	47%	187	92%
ENCD	ENCAD		6-May	200	STOCK	19	$ 3,800.00	25-Feb	32 7/8	$ 6,575.00	$ 2,775.00	73%	296	90%
MER	MERRILL LYNCH		14-Feb	5	MAR 95	5 7/8	$ 2,937.50	18-Feb	7 3/4	$ 3,875.00	$ 937.50	32%	4	2,912%
KEY	KEY PRODUCTION		30-Sep	100	STOCK	44 1/8	$ 4,412.50	25-Feb	56	$ 5,600.00	$ 1,187.50	27%	149	66%
T	AT&T		30-Jan	5	MAR 35	5	$ 2,500.00	25-Feb	6	$ 3,000.00	$ 500.00	20%	27	270%
APPI	ADV. PLANT PHARM	BOTTOMFISH	23-Dec	20K	STOCK	4/25	$ 3,200.00	26-Feb	6/25	$ 4,800.00	$ 1,600.00	50%	65	281%
CSN	CINCINATTI BELL	SPLT ANNCD	3-Feb	500	STOCK	62 1/2	$ 31,250.00	25-Feb	64 1/8	$ 32,062.50	$ 812.50	3%	22	43%
STT	STATE STREET	SPLT ANNCD	20-Feb	5	MAY 85	5 5/8	$ 2,812.50	25-Feb	6 3/4	$ 3,375.00	$ 562.50	20%	5	1,460%

These are some of our most recent trades. Obviously, your returns may be different. Trades listed here are no guarantee of future success. Annualized returns are listed for comparison purposes only. We acknowledge that these are short (3-hour, 3-week, or 3-month) plays and that the same money is not continually invested at all times. We listed the actual date and purchase prices so you could verify the trades. You should check with your own professionals regarding the risks and rewards in your personal account. U.S.A. Inc, Wade Cook and the instructors make no recommendations and give no advice. We teach correct methods and strategies and let people govern their own transactions -- and keep their own profits!

TICKER	COMPANY	REASON	BUY DATE	QTY	POSITION	PRICE	TOTAL	SELL DATE	PRICE	TOTAL IN	GAIN/LOSS	%	DAYS	ANN %
STT	STATE STREET	SPLT ANNCD	6-Mar	5	APR 80	3 7/8	$ 1,937.50	10-Mar	4 7/8	$ 2,437.50	$ 500.00	26%	4	2,355%
CL	COLGATE PALMOLIVE	SPLT ANNCD	6-Mar	10	APR 105	6 5/8	$ 6,625.00	7-Mar	7 1/4	$ 7,250.00	$ 625.00	9%	1	3,443%
MCAF	MC AFEE		6-Mar	5	APR 50 P	3 1/2	$ 1,750.00	10-Mar	5 1/2	$ 2,750.00	$ 1,000.00	57%	4	5,214%
BA	BOEING		25-Feb	5	MAR 105	5/8	$ 312.50	3-Mar	1 11/16	$ 843.75	$ 531.25	170%	6	10,342%
CL	COLGATE PALMOLIVE	SPLT ANNCD	6-Mar	5	MAR 105	4 1/2	$ 2,250.00	6-Mar	5 1/8	$ 2,562.50	$ 312.50	14%	1	5,069%
BAC	BANK AMERICA		4-Mar	20	APR 120	3 1/2	$ 7,000.00	6-Mar	4 1/2	$ 9,000.00	$ 2,000.00	29%	2	5,214%
WX	WESTINGHOUSE		20-Feb	10	APR 17.50	1 3/16	$ 1,187.50	6-Mar	2 1/4	$ 2,250.00	$ 1,062.50	89%	14	2,333%
KM	K-MART		14-Jan	1000	STOCK	11	$ 11,000.00	5-Mar	13 1/8	$ 13,125.00	$ 2,125.00	19%	40	176%
DD	DUPONT	SPLT ANNCD	3-Mar	10	JUL 110	6	$ 6,000.00	3-Mar	7	$ 7,000.00	$ 1,000.00	17%	1	6,083%
BOBJY	BUSINESS OBJECTS	COV CALL	4-Mar	3	MAR 12.50	1/4	$ 75.00	13-Feb	1 5/16	$ 393.60	$ 318.60	425%	19	8,161%
WX	WESTINGHOUSE		21-Feb	10	JUL 17.50	1 3/4	$ 1,750.00	6-Mar	2 1/4	$ 2,250.00	$ 500.00	29%	13	802%
OREM	OREGONMETALURGICAL		5-Feb	10	MAR 22.50	3 1/8	$ 3,125.00	10-Mar	7/16	$ 437.50	$ (2,687.50)	-86%	33	-951%
STT	STATE STREET	SPLT ANNCD	20-Feb	10	MAR 85	2 3/8	$ 2,375.00	20-Feb	3 1/2	$ 3,500.00	$ 1,125.00	47%	1	17,289%
SHBZ	SHOWBIZ PIZZA	SPLIT PLAY	22-Apr	150	STOCK	14 1/2	$ 2,175.00	25-Feb	20 3/4	$ 3,112.50	$ 937.50	43%	300	52%
U	US AIR		17-Oct	1000	STOCK	16 1/4	$ 16,250.00	25-Feb	20	$ 20,000.00	$ 3,750.00	23%	131	64%
CL	COLGATE PALMOLIVE	SPLT ANNCD	6-Mar	10	APR 110	4 3/4	$ 4,750.00	7-Mar	5 1/2	$ 5,500.00	$ 750.00	16%	1	5,763%
GE	GENERAL ELECTRIC		3-Mar	20	APR 100	5 3/4	$ 11,500.00	7-Mar	7 3/4	$ 15,500.00	$ 4,000.00	35%	4	3,174%
BAC	BANK AMERICA	NAKED PUT	7-Mar	10	MAR 115 P	1	$ 1,000.00	3-Mar	2 3/8	$ 2,375.00	$ 1,375.00	138%	4	12,547%
PG	PROCTER & GAMBLE		7-Mar	5	JUL 125	5 3/4	$ 2,875.00	11-Mar	9	$ 4,500.00	$ 1,625.00	57%	4	5,158%
KMB	KIMBERLY CLARK		7-Mar	3	APR 105	5	$ 1,500.00	11-Mar	6 5/8	$ 1,987.50	$ 487.50	33%	4	2,966%
NB	NATION'S BANK		27-Feb	8	MAR 60 P	3	$ 2,400.00	10-Mar	4 1/4	$ 3,400.00	$ 1,000.00	42%	11	1,383%

These are some of our most recent trades. Obviously, your returns may be different. Trades listed here are no guarantee of future success. Annualized returns are listed for comparison purposes only. We acknowledge that these are short (3-hour, 3-week, or 3-month) plays and that the same money is not continually invested at all times. We listed the actual date and purchase prices so you could verify the trades. You should check with your own professionals regarding the risks and rewards in your personal account. U.S.A. Inc, Wade Cook and the instructors make no recommendations and give no advice. We teach correct methods and strategies and let people govern their own transactions -- and keep their own profits!

TICKER	COMPANY	REASON	BUY DATE	QTY	POSITION	PRICE	TOTAL	SELL DATE	PRICE	TOTAL IN	GAIN/LOSS	%	DAY	ANN. %
OEX	S & P 100		18-Mar	5	MAR 770 P	6 7/8	$ 3,437.50	18-Mar	8 1/4	$ 4,125.00	$ 687.50	20%	1	7,300%
FOTO	SEATTLE FILM WORKS	NAKED PUT	18-Mar	5	APR 11.625	7/8	$ 437.50	13-Mar	1 1/8	$ 562.50	$ 125.00	29%	5	2,086%
CPB	CAMPBELL SOUP	STK SPLT	14-Mar	10	MAR 45	1 3/4	$ 1,750.00	18-Mar	2 1/16	$ 2,062.00	$ 312.00	18%	4	1,627%
KO	COCA COLA	COV CALL	12-Mar	10	MAR 60	1	$ 1,000.00	20-Feb	2 1/2	$ 2,500.00	$ 1,500.00	150%	20	2,738%
PG	PROCTER & GAMBLE	NEWS	26-Feb	10	APR 120	6	$ 6,000.00	14-Mar	6 7/8	$ 6,875.00	$ 875.00	15%	16	333%
BAC	BANK AMERICA	STK SPLT	25-Feb	5	AUG 110	7 3/4	$ 3,875.00	12-Mar	8 1/8	$ 4,062.50	$ 187.50	5%	15	118%
PG	PROCTER & GAMBLE	NEWS	7-Mar	15	JUL 125	6 1/4	$ 9,375.00	14-Mar	8 1/4	$ 12,375.00	$ 3,000.00	32%	7	1,669%
BA	BOEING		2-Dec	500	STOCK	98 1/4	$ 49,125.00	12-Mar	107 7/8	$ 53,937.50	$ 4,812.50	10%	100	36%
PG	PROCTER & GAMBLE	NEWS	7-Mar	10	APR 125	2 3/4	$ 2,750.00	10-Mar	4	$ 4,000.00	$ 1,250.00	45%	3	5,530%
PG	PROCTER & GAMBLE	NEWS	7-Mar	15	APR 125	2 15/16	$ 4,406.25	14-Mar	4 1/8	$ 6,187.50	$ 1,781.25	40%	7	2,108%
PG	PROCTER & GAMBLE	NEWS	7-Mar	10	JUL 120	8 3/4	$ 8,750.00	14-Mar	11 1/4	$ 11,250.00	$ 2,500.00	29%	7	1,490%
EUGS	EUROGAS	BRKR REC.	30-Jan	5500	STOCK	4 1/32	$ 22,172.15	12-Mar	6 3/8	$ 35,062.50	$ 12,890.35	58%	41	518%
PG	PROCTER & GAMBLE	NEWS	7-Mar	5	JUL 125	5 3/4	$ 2,875.00	11-Mar	9	$ 4,500.00	$ 1,625.00	57%	4	5,158%
PG	PROCTER & GAMBLE	NEWS	7-Mar	10	JUL 130	4 1/2	$ 4,500.00	10-Mar	6	$ 6,000.00	$ 1,500.00	33%	3	4,056%
PG	PROCTER & GAMBLE	NEWS	7-Mar	5	APR 120	5 1/4	$ 2,625.00	10-Mar	6 1/2	$ 3,250.00	$ 625.00	24%	3	2,897%
UNM	UNUM	STK SPLT	14-Mar	5	APR 80	7/8	$ 437.50	14-Mar	1 1/2	$ 750.00	$ 312.50	71%	1	26,071%
ZITL	ZITEL	NAKED PUT	13-Mar	5	MAR 30	1 1/16	$ 531.00	5-Mar	2 5/8	$ 1,312.50	$ 781.50	147%	8	6,715%
PG	PROCTER & GAMBLE	NEWS	7-Mar	5	JUL 125	5 3/4	$ 2,875.00	11-Mar	9	$ 4,500.00	$ 1,625.00	57%	4	5,158%
KL	KIMBERLY CLARK	STK SPLT	7-Mar	3	APR 105	5	$ 1,500.00	11-Mar	6 5/8	$ 1,987.50	$ 487.50	33%	4	2,966%

These are some of our most recent trades. Obviously, your returns may be different. Your returns may be different. Trades listed here are no guarantee of future success. Annualized returns are listed for comparison purposes only. We acknowledge that these are short (3-hour, 3-week, or 3-month) plays and that the same money is not continually invested at all times. We listed the actual date and purchase prices so you could verify the trades. You should check with your own professionals regarding the risks and rewards in your personal account. U.S.A. Inc, Wade Cook and the instructors make no recommendations and give no advice. We teach correct methods and strategies and let people govern their own transactions – and keep their own profits!

Press on.
Nothing in the world
can take the place of persistence.
Talent will not:
nothing is more common than
unrewarded talent.
Education alone is not enough:
the world is full of educated failures.
Persistence alone is omnipotent.
—Calvin Coolidge